Thoughts and Words
Reflections on Child Welfare
and Other Topics

Thoughts and Words
Reflections on Child Welfare and Other Topics

Charles P. Conroy

Angus MacGregor Books

Angus MacGregor Books
75 Green Street
Clinton MA 01510

Copyright © 2007 by Charles P. Conroy

All rights reserved, including the right to reproduce this book or portions thereof in any form whatsoever.
For Information address Angus MacGregor Books, 75 Green Street, Clinton MA 01510.

ISBN: **0-9790598-3-6**
ISBN 13: **978-0-9790598-3-4**

First Angus MacGregor Books softcover edition January 2007

10 9 8 7 6 5 4 3 2 1

Angus MacGregor Books

For information regarding special discounts for bulk purchases please contact Angus MacGregor Books, Print Sales Department or
email: printsales@booktrauma.com

Printed and Manufactured in the United States of America

Table of Contents

Foreword 2
Introduction: I'm A Parent Too! 4

2001-2002
Terrorist Attacks "Unfathomable" 25
A Christmas Foster Care Story 27
Commencement Address (2002) Anna Maria College 30
"Yuh-huh" 36
"Sleep With The Light On" 39

2003-2004
The Nun Was Right 45
Perkins 1987-2003: A Report 52
"The Sea We Carry Within Us" 59
The Fallacy of Inevitability 62
Not Even Geoghan Deserved "Punishment" He Met in Prison 67
A Peculiar Breed Indeed 69
Not Filling A Bucket, But Lighting a Fire" 71
Keeping Babies Out of the River 74
New Challenges, New Directions 88

2005-2006
Should Residential Program Staff Become Adoptive, Foster, or Visiting Resources for Children in Their Programs? 97
Why Catholic Education? 100
Encouragement 109
Urges Good-bye to the Good Ole Days 113
They'll Remember How We Made Them Feel 116
Administrators Need to Use Their Brains 123
The Wrong Way to Reform Child Welfare 125
Your World, Your Community, and You 127
"It's Never Too Late To Be What You Might Have Been." 134
Perseverance, Risk-Taking, and Building Bridges 137

Eulogies
Charles P. Conroy, Sr. 1920-2002 147
Katherine E. Perkins 1927-2005 152
Sonja Bernier 1940-2006 155

Foreword

I am not sure that this volume picks up where the previous one left off, but that's probably not too far from accurate. However, the thrust is a bit different. This book is less informational and maybe more emotional, more "heart" than "head," because it has a lot of my reactions and observations about what's going on with kids rather than a compilation of facts and data accumulated by others. However, it does contain a bit of an update on several of the issues children face and that's found in the talk titled, "Keeping Babies Out of the River."

In the introductory essay, "I'm a Parent Too!" I try to review some of the experiences I've had as a foster parent, a status I took on shortly after the publication of *"Who's Throwing Babies in the River?* in 2001. What follows that piece are some other essays, published newspaper or journal articles, and speeches I have given since 2001.

In these pieces I allude to the change (or, more accurately the lack of change) in the condition of children in the interim. I have chosen not to pursue an in-depth, laborious five-year follow up of each of the topics found in the first book. I don't think that things are dramatically different. Some conditions are worse and some are marginally better. An update would not prove particularly fruitful.

So, what you have in front of you is a collection of writings and presentations for a variety of audiences – the general public, the staff at Perkins School, child welfare professionals, school health personnel, a college graduation class, a high school graduation class, a chamber of commerce group, and students at Perkins, a school for mentally ill, neglected, and abused kids, that I have headed since 1987. I have also included pieces published in newspapers or journals on topics related to our work at Perkins and a few previously unpublished essays.

They are all arranged chronologically rather than topically and can be read in any order the reader chooses. Perkins also provides services to adults and elderly people with special needs, who I number among my close friends and associates, but who (maybe thankfully) are not the focus of this book that focuses on issues related to the children we serve.

The last three pieces are eulogies. Two of them were actually delivered and the other one was sent to the family because there was such a huge outpouring of sentiment by a large number of eulogists that this one might well have proved redundant. All three individuals were exemplary people I have been privileged to know. They were amazing people in their own ways and they affected many others, although they had very different styles.

I wish to express my sincere thanks to my bosses, the Board of Trustees of Perkins, a group that has provided direction and leadership to the organization over the course of these almost 20 years. They have simultaneously offered encouragement and support to me personally. I remain deeply indebted to the staff at Perkins and to my colleagues, the dedicated human service professionals and teachers I meet all the time.

I add to the gratitude I expressed in the first book to my daughters, Melissa and Janet, a similar thanks to my foster son, Jay, who reminds me every day how important and rewarding it is for adults to see kids grow and progress. That's what makes it all worthwhile. He also gives me great material! I reiterate my admiration and thanks to David Dunn of Dunn & Co. and Legacy Publishing Group for his ongoing encouragement and support.

We are living through a period when some of the basic services we offer at Perkins and in other residential facilities are being critiqued for philosophically sound child welfare reasons. Sometimes, however, the analysis and criticism are driven by fiscal concerns couched in philosophical platitudes that barely conceal the true intent of the critics.

We face such challenges in child welfare circles periodically because of the need to balance child protection with keeping families together or reunifying them after they have come apart. I continue to embrace the belief that children, especially vulnerable and wounded children, need to be protected. I believe that is a primary obligation of government. I also believe in the paramount importance of family and its primacy in nurturing and fostering growth and healthy development in children. Maybe that's why I'm a foster parent.

Fiscal constraints, while a realistic fact of life, do not relieve us of the responsibility to ensure the safety and welfare of children who cannot protect themselves. The technocrats and "re-engineers" of government for all their theorizing sometimes fail to realize that. Until the *sources* of problems are ameliorated, we will collectively continue to wander in the desert of "quick fixes" to age-old problems that will never be completely fixed.

The problems should be prevented not just fixed. At the moment we remain firmly stationed on the riverbanks plucking babies out of the water, rather than strategically moving upstream to ensure that they are never tossed into the river at all.

Introduction: I'm a Parent Too!

2001-2006

Who's Throwing Babies in the River was published in December 2001, a few months after the 9/11 attacks on the World Trade Center in New York City and the Pentagon and the crash of a fourth hijacked airliner in Pennsylvania. I briefly alluded to the attacks in the first chapter of the book to put into perspective the evolutionary problem of the condition of children and the imminent, dramatic threat posed by the terrorists.

They both continue in virtually unchanged patterns. One is stagnant and the other continues to grow. Children's issues have not moved to the forefront of social concerns. Since 9/11, Spain and London have been terrorist targets. A plot to explode airliners over the Atlantic Ocean was exposed in the Summer of 2006 and, as a result, even more stringent rules have been put in place regarding air travel.

Since 2001 and the publication of the first book, I have continued to monitor the condition of children in the United States and to write and to speak on topics related to kids, particularly kids with unique needs – abused kids, incarcerated kids, and mentally ill kids. There continue to be bright spots amid the challenges. However, many of the bright spots are the kids themselves. Their resilience and ability to overcome tragic histories and move forward with optimism and hope that the future will be better than the past are most encouraging.

I see very little evidence of a national commitment or agenda to address child poverty, homelessness, abuse, neglect, health and mental health. Where there has been renewed interest in education it is mostly confined to standardized, "high stakes" testing as a prerequisite for grade advancement rather than attention to social and emotional learning, how children learn, and how we can best teach them. The evolving national agenda and federal control of education is frightening given the localized, state-supervised pattern that had existed in this country from its very foundations. "No Child Left Behind" has a wonderfully sonorous ring to it, but the reality is that many kids are left behind every day and many more will continue to be.

Foster Parent

My perspective on the overall conditions children face in our country has changed little. However, in the five intervening years since the publication of the first book, I have taken on another role, one very different from the previous positions, jobs, and responsibilities I've had for the previous 30 years. In the spring of 2002 I became a "visiting resource" to three brothers, ages seven, eight, and ten years old, who had been students for the previous year and half at the Perkins School, the school program of a large central Massachusetts human service organization where I have lived and worked since 1987. Later on, I became foster father to the same three brothers.

I'm not a strong believer in life changing experiences. I think that people pursue their lives based on beliefs, routines, upbringing, inclinations, talents, things that bring them pleasure, and, I suppose, genetic disposition to some extent. I see value in both sides of the nature-nurture dichotomy and think neither is the sole determinant of who we are or why we do what we do. I believe that nature *and* nurture, genes *and* environment, play key roles in who we become as adults.

However, I cannot deny that some experiences can come dangerously close to being life transforming, or at least life shaping, because they widen our horizons, expand our perspectives, and generally enable us to think or see things in ways we never have before. Such has been my odyssey as a foster parent.

I view kids in group care, foster care, and therapeutic foster care differently now than I did before I experienced the policies, practices and ways of doing business of the child welfare bureaucracy (aka "the system"). In that bureaucracy I have encountered some of the most dedicated and committed professionals you are likely to meet. I've also met some traditional "dinosaurs" who deal with foster parents in a condescending, high-handed manner. This latter group long ago lost sight of the centrality of kids in the whole process of guaranteeing children's safety, ensuring their welfare, and providing what's best for them. Thankfully, the former vastly outnumber the latter.

I have added to my personal and professional perspectives an outlook I simply did not possess prior to meeting the three foster sons (and, later, their oldest brother whom I got to know pretty well). As of this writing only one of the boys remains with me in my home, but we all have regular contact. This experience has resulted in this initial essay, *"I'm a Parent Too,"* which is then followed by a number of talks, essays, and presentations. The pieces following are a bit more lighthearted than this one which is the "up and down" story of my foster care experience.

For a lot of reasons, some of which had as much to do with me as with them, the three brothers only lasted together in my home for about three months. The middle brother, now 13 years old, has been with me since October 2002.

He does more than merely grow. He is blossoming socially, academically, athletically, and developmentally. He's got friends, male and, more recently, female and that's great. Physically, he isn't doing badly either. At 11 years of age he hit 173 lbs. and a height of 5' 6"! He's big, but he can still move pretty swiftly across a lacrosse field, throw a palm-burning fast ball, and, man, is he ever strong. So far, I've won the arm wrestling contests, but that won't last for long.

A Different Perspective

As a foster parent, I have been able to see the child welfare/foster care system from the inside. Because I worked in a totally different part of the child welfare system - residential and day treatment – I really didn't know what foster care was all about. Some of the pieces that follow this one contain vignettes, anecdotes, and stories that are a direct result of my new role as foster father. That experience, as you will read, has not been without its lighter moments.

Being a parent to my own daughters was certainly a help as I got further into this, but in a lot of ways I was in uncharted waters. You end up negotiating your way in this system very differently than the systems and processes you experience with your own children. The foster parent-foster child relationship and experiences are not the same as those you encounter raising your own children. Anyone who tells you differently is wrong - pure and simple.

It's not the "boy-girl thing" that made it different. I raised two girls, but I am the oldest of five brothers, so I know something about males. I also had taught in an all-boys high school and supervised and administered programs for kids with special needs, disproportionately boys by the way, for a long time.

Three years ago at the age of 54, I bought a speedboat, something I had managed to avoid for all the earlier years of my life. My foster parent job description has now been expanded to include dragging kids around a lake on skis, wakeboard, or tube. The acquisition of the boat itself suggests something of a transformation in my outlook and behavior. I've even taken my turn on the rope swing attached to the big pine tree overlooking the lake.

I never had the slightest desire to own or operate any kind of watercraft until I was able to see opportunities for these three guys to acquire new skills, attain a greater level of responsibility, and uncover some athletic abilities that they never knew they had. Acquiring the boat in some ways is comparable to my foster care decision. Getting the boat came about after soul-searching, assessment, evaluation, and, I hope, informed decision-making. That's how the decision to become a foster parent was made as well.

Throughout my foster parent experience, I have been able to see that "normalization," i.e., getting kids who experience some degree of problems, difficulties, and isolation back into the mainstream in their communities, is, indeed, a worthwhile objective. My father used to say that you can buy or get a kid just about anything, but you can't get them friends. He was right. Kids need other kids. Being involved in the community, playing little league baseball or lacrosse, or just riding your bike around town with the guys is a major feature of growing up, feeling accepted, being "normal," and experiencing some degree of success and independence.

I owe a great debt to local parents who took my foster son to practices and games when other demands on me made it impossible. Along the way I have gotten to know them, when otherwise I never would have. I have come to see that young parents of the early 21st century, who stand on the sidelines at their kids' games, just as us parents of the earlier generation did in the 80's and 90's, have many similar goals - but some of the attitudes and conversation seem to have evolved.

My white hair tends to exclude me somewhat from the group, but that's fine. Mere contact with these younger parents has helped me to understand their attitudes about kids. At my age I can also respond in ways that might be different. At a frigid April lacrosse practice in what people euphemistically refer to as "spring" in New England, one parent vowed to show up at the next game with "coffee and Bailey's Irish Cream." My response was very simply, "to hell with the coffee."

Sure, every once in a while someone will ask if "grandpa" likes coming to the kid's games. But – you know what? He does!

Kids in "The System"

More and more we are coming to the conclusion that academic success is tied to emotional and social development and growth and I have seen evidence of this over and over again. Happy kids, well adjusted kids, maybe even carefree kids (if there are any in 2006!) simply go about life's tasks in ways than ensure their ultimate success. They have positive, optimistic outlooks that carry over into all they do.

For many kids in "the system" the deck is stacked against them since the happiness that is the hallmark of success remains an elusive goal itself. The system doesn't consciously make kids miserable, but it doesn't do enough to enable them to secure the degree of happiness they need to view life as something worth living and participating in with the energy and enthusiasm that it requires.

Too many of these kids lose heart, give up, and become lifelong recipients of care rather givers of care. Too many end up in correctional facilities or other institutions. Too few become successful parents, productive, self-sufficient workers, and satisfied, invested citizens.

Some of that happens because we don't invest in kids early. We don't make the most dramatic intervention early enough, even when it's clear it's needed. Rather, we try the "band-aid" approach.

Kids "fail up." They only get the more intensive treatment levels of the system after they have failed in the less intensive ones in the hierarchy below. We don't do enough at prevention and, when we do get around to intervention, it's often too little, too late. What results are long periods of time in care, maybe even lifetimes in care.

A state official in Massachusetts not too long ago insensitively reduced people to being "givers" and "takers" based on economic condition. A blizzard of criticism justifiably followed. That's not at all the distinction

I'm making. I'm referring to being able to give – to render care, show emotion, experience empathy, even love others. I sometimes feel, admittedly somewhat simplistically, that "you can't give it, if you haven't gotten it." Some of these kids haven't gotten it.

Kids in the system often lack the proper role models for empathy and compassion and some have rarely seen healthy displays of affection and devotion to family. They move from placement to placement, program to program, and through the hands and care of very sincere and dedicated professionals and foster parents - but they do not get what they need emotionally.

In the vast majority of cases, their basic needs - food, clothing and shelter - are met. However, all too often we are treated to a media-circus, feeding frenzy when a child in a group care program or foster care is injured or dies. Focus for a moment on the fact that such tragedies represent a very small percentage of those in care and make up an infinitesimal percentage of children generally.

The standard the media applies to group care or foster care is very different than that applied to biological parents when exactly the same kind of tragedy occurs in a natural family. The old news media axiom that "if it bleeds, it leads" seems to be directed much more vigorously to kids in out-of-home situations than those in biological families.

That is something I probably would not have said five years ago, but not because I didn't have the perspective of group care as being vilified by the news media. As a CEO of a child welfare organization, I certainly did. However as a foster parent, it has become clear to me that "whipping boy" status for group care and foster parents is just too tempting for the media to pass up. Forget the fact that the incidence of abuse in natural families is markedly *greater* than group or foster care.

"Out-of-Home" Kids Need More

While basic needs for kids in group care and foster care are met in almost all cases, that's not good enough. In 2006, kids who come out of group and foster care must be more than simply well-cared for if they are to experience anything approaching a successful, fulfilled existence. They certainly need, first and foremost, love and nurturance. However, they must also have social skills, life skills, and the proper schooling and that must include being technologically prepared at school and at home.

Kids in group and foster care must also have access to computers so they can surf the Internet, navigate the Web, use e-mail, and do all the things their "normal" counterparts in natural families can do. If they don't, they will become "sore thumbs" and stick out very obviously as adolescents and adults.

I would go so far as to say that every kid in group care or foster care should have his or her own laptop or at least access to a home desktop computer. Not to be technologically fluent ensures failure later on.

Providing kids with the proper technological experiences also means that the adults supervising them will have their lives become more complicated since they have to monitor what the kids are doing.

E-mail, instant messaging, Xanga, and My Space are great ways for kids to be connected to others, but they present some huge challenges as well. It seems that not a day goes by that we don't hear about some adult trying to take advantage of a kid on the Internet. Most recently, there was a congressman who wrote inappropriate e-mails to congressional pages. Foster parents – *all* parents - have to be vigilant.

I'm not sure I would take the same position as far as cell phones are concerned. I am not so sure every kid should have one, but parents should know that there are great residual benefits from kids having them – for the parents as well as the kids. I can find my foster son anytime I want to. He's rarely out of my sight and less rarely out of my mind, so it helps for me to have instant cell phone access when he's out of earshot.

Why Be a Foster Parent?

It may be instructive to review my own experience as a foster parent because I think there are a lot of people who have flirted with the idea of becoming one but heard too many horror stories to go much further. I am not prepared to say there are no obstacles and that it's smooth sailing right from the start, but if you're willing to put up with the frustrations you encounter with any bureaucracy, ultimately you will triumph.

We usually come out of the Registry of Motor Vehicles with our license and registration, the goal when we went in. Sometimes it's not easy and it's rarely pleasant, but it's not supposed to be. It takes time and you have to understand and conform to the rules – but eventually you get what you came for. There's not a lot of smiles in the process, but the lady behind window #14 at the RMV wasn't told to be charming, just to get the job done. You have to go through the process to get what you want.

The early foster care credentialing experience is similar. Don't look for gratification or a lot of touchy-feely, "I think this is so nice what you're doing"-types of people. You won't find many. Some people you'll run into have been hardened by years of seeing kids mistreated and you have to understand that. You're a potential foster parent and ally - but you're a potential "perp" too - at least until your criminal record check comes back!

If you're committed to seeing it through, enduring a period of investigation you might find intrusive and demoralizing from time to time, and absolutely believe in kids and your own strengths in being able to care for them, it's worth pursuing foster parenting. However, I'm not going to lie to you, the process is not for the faint of heart. And, yes, a lot of people will think you just did it for the money.

If you don't like people asking a lot of questions, snooping around your house, and generally intruding on your privacy, don't volunteer for foster care. If you can put up with all those (and, frankly, it's really not that bad!), then do it. Some kid will be better off as a result.

My Experience

Anyway, here's how it went for me. When I think back to how and why I made the decision to become a foster parent, I inevitably arrive at a question that the youngest of the three brothers, the seven-year-old, put to me early on.

"Why d'ya pick us?" he asked.

That's a great question by the way. Of the hundreds, maybe thousands, of kids I've come in contact with, why did I make the decision to foster parent these three guys? The easy answer is that they represented one of the most compelling cases I had encountered in all my years of education, special education, and child welfare.

Without violating confidentiality (and throughout this piece I have been very careful not to use names other than a pseudonym for my current foster son), let me just say that these three kids came from backgrounds where abuse and neglect had been alleged. A number of people, including teachers, had documented the neglect and lack of supervision. The state Department of Social Services (DSS) got involved and ultimately took custody of all the boys, but parental rights were not terminated.

The other thing that bothered me was that, if the three were discharged from Perkins separately, they might never have seen each other again. They already hadn't seen their oldest brother in several years! My hope was to keep them together in the same home, have them go to public school, and generally grow up together.

So, those were my two initial goals: helping them overcome their past and keeping them together for the future. To some extent that has happened, although not the way I planned – but more about that later.

I went through the "home study" phase of the process, filled out endless forms, and had a variety of conversations with staff of DSS and the subcontracting foster care agency. I live on the campus of Perkins and one would presume that the environment would be child-friendly and free of obvious dangers to kids. This phase moved quickly.

I also have my own home about six miles from the campus that I use mostly weekends and summers. It also was deemed safe, although I think if the powers that be had their way they would have moved the lake that is contiguous to the property.

The reason there was a subcontractor involved rather than dealing directly with DSS was that Massachusetts contracts out for "specialized," "therapeutic," or "intensive" foster care, i.e., care for kids who have greater needs than the average kid in state care. Specialized foster care also has rules and regulations unique to it based on the belief that kids with more complicated needs also require a closer degree of supervision. On the surface that sounds eminently sensible.

The Rules

A lot of the regulations are reasonable, but some of them are simply rooted in bad experiences of the past. They have found their way into the rulebook so that DSS or contracting agencies aren't embarrassed if a tragedy occurs under circumstances similar to a previous one. The system cringes at the possibility that someone will say, "You mean you didn't learn from that experience three years ago. Now *this* happens and it's exactly the same thing." The media enjoys taking that approach.

You probably didn't realize that, if you own a pit bull, Rottweiler or German Shepherd, you can't take a foster child into your home. No one has ever confirmed for me that it's because the last three kids who were mauled or killed in foster care were mauled by pit bulls, Rottweilers or German Shepherds, but that's my guess. I don't believe that anyone actually did a study to ascertain which dog breeds are the most likely to attack kids and then proceeded to put *those* prohibited breeds into the regulations. That would make sense.

I figure these three breeds were picked because there had been bad experiences with them earlier. Insurance companies ask similar kinds of questions and they have some "high risk" breeds as well.

I later heard that the breed of dog that bites the most kids is – are you ready for this? – Golden Retrievers. Why aren't Goldens on the foster care hit list? I don't want to bore you with a lot of statistical data, but I'm going to guess that it's true because there are simply more golden retrievers in households with kids across the United States. That would almost ensure that there would be more Golden Retriever bites.

State child welfare departments often don't do sophisticated statistical analysis prior to establishing policy, procedures, or regulations. They simply react to the last tragedy and practice the time-honored philosophy of "covering themselves." The way you do that is to develop a list that focuses on the dogs that have given you trouble in the past, but who are not necessarily the ones who statistically present the greatest danger. It may not have the safest result for kids, but, from a defensive standpoint, at least you won't look foolish again.

By the way, throughout all the studies, interviews, home tours, and cabinet checks in both my houses, the home study staff and I were accompanied by Isaiah - my 12-year-old Golden Retriever! He has since passed on to his great reward, his record untarnished and his breed not sullied by state bureaucrats - a fitting conclusion to a long and happy life of 14 years. I think, if asked, he would have expressed his opinion that German Shepherds are getting a raw deal.

I was also informed during the home study that certain household items needed to be locked up. Over the counter medications and alcohol of any kind were verboten and needed to be kept in a locked cabinet. A cold beer in the refrigerator for a friend or neighbor who might drop by? No!

(Guess they have to drink it warm unless you have one of those expensive, locked wine coolers.)

The previous year my daughters had given me a winemaking kit and I had gone through the process and bottled about 2½ cases of wine. I had them displayed in beautiful, cast iron wine racks. Do they have to go? You betcha! Lock 'em up.

I suggested at one point that maybe if I just kept the corkscrew under wraps, the threat would be minimal. No good. I put forth the idea that any kid who needed to crack the top off a bottle and suck down a bottle of wine probably wasn't ready for any kind of foster care.

No good. Do what you're told.

I wondered aloud about the real degree of danger presented by a corked bottle of wine, a vial of Tylenol, or a roll of Tums versus the 10-piece set of knives I had on the kitchen counter. An errant foster child could easily disembowel, pare, carve, and dice me if he chose using the knife of choice. However, the knives were simply not on the list of proscribed items. But keep that Ex-Lax under lock and key! Ludicrous.

This whole issue later became something of a bone of contention as part of a larger discussion I had with the foster care managers. I maintained then (and now) that kids in specialized foster care must be able to see progress and that the "one size fits all" approach didn't let them see when they were getting better.

If you come into specialized foster care at eight years old, you are subject to the same regulations when you leave at eighteen. You will always live in a house where the aspirin and beer are locked up. The foster care staff made it very clear they were not interested in negotiating based on a child's record, positive experiences, and excellent demeanor. (You can even attain "trustee" status in prison!)

I think kids need to be able to see progress and be subject to rules and regulations that support progress. A system designed first and foremost to cover those who administer it, rather than a system based on the kids in its care, is a system designed to fail.

Kids won't get better if they see no progress, no end in sight, and no light at the end of the tunnel. It's also why some kids never leave the system or, why, when they do, they later become dependent adults.

The foster care enforcers weren't totally intransigent and inflexible when it came to some rules. We were later able to agree that the foster son who is still with me, Jay, can be alone in the house for an hour. I had to actively work to have him complete weekly therapy sessions that were totally useless, that he hated, and that substantively had no value for anyone. I recently heard that another foster child was able to have some unsupervised time. We may be making some advances after all. We have to look at individual needs, concentrate on individual strengths, and be somewhat flexible.

When the three brothers were all in therapy (a logistical and transportation nightmare by the way!), the central issue for the therapist seemed to be that they "teased" each other. Given their history, teasing hadn't made it anywhere near the top of my list. I would have probed a little at their feelings of abandonment and the sequelae to their alleged abuse, but what do I know, I'm just a foster parent!

The psychiatrist we consulted was an expert. She was engaging, and totally agreed that, as progress was made, the medication regimen could be reviewed and, where indicated, adjusted. Within a year of his moving in to my house, Jay, the middle brother, was off all medication. This was more than a glimmer of hope.

A Crisis: It's All Off!

But I've moved too quickly in the story. Let me back up a bit. When I was finally approved as a foster parent, we began the process of developing a schedule for the three boys to move in. Spring passed into summer and we were looking to do it in order of age, having oldest to youngest move in on a staggered schedule. (As it turned out later, that was not to be the case. The middle brother came first, then the youngest, then the oldest.)

All was going along fine. In the summer reality began to set in and I asked some questions about support they might give me. I knew I would need a second pair of hands in the house. I had never been deeply involved in the foster care system and hadn't even yet had any discussion about compensation because, frankly, it wasn't what motivated me to do any of this. All of my experience until that time had been in a different part of the child welfare field. I knew little of the economic terms for foster parents.

When I raised the question of assistance, the response was startling. Someone must have thought I was angling for money. I didn't even know what kind of reimbursement was involved. When I asked the question about hiring someone to assist me, I had no idea that what they were going to reimburse me for specialized foster care would easily cover hiring someone.

I could get someone to help me with laundry, homework and the general needs of three boys for several hours a day. (I ultimately did hire a young lady who was fantastic. She had worked at Perkins, knew the kinds of kids we had, and she wasn't easily pushed around. She stayed with us for all the time I had the three boys and finished when two of them went to other placements.)

But – back to the bureaucratic response to my inquiry. When I naively asked about help, a supervisor in DSS immediately reacted and decided to call the whole thing off. Worst of all, she sent the case worker out to Perkins to tell the boys that "they weren't going to Dr. Conroy's house."

I was dumbfounded, angry, and wasted no time in responding. This sent me into orbit and managed to surface all the old, bad stereotypes I had about DSS from my past professional experience. I was working real hard to dispel those negative images in this process, but they weren't making it easy.

To my request for help came a response that DSS simply wasn't going to move ahead with placements. They were just going to end the whole thing right there and then. Had they told me that directly, we could have sat down and spoken and ascertained what the problem with the request was. They resorted to the raw use of power. That wouldn't ordinarily bother me if they were simply coming after me, but they chose the cowardly way out. They were using the kids.

I felt that to use the boys as "pawns" to negotiate me down or push me around was unconscionable and I told everyone that – the ombudsman for DSS, the DSS worker, the supervisor, the Commissioner's office, and the DSS Area Director. The Area Director, as it turned out, was a charming, polished, and savvy professional, nothing like the mindless bureaucrat stereotype that unfairly plagues state workers. I also shared my predicament with my local state representative and state senator.

We eventually were able to get the whole thing back on track when they explained that they were not going to give me direct "staff" assistance but that the reimbursement I would receive could easily be used for that purpose. Case closed.

I was pleased with the outcome. What they were going to reimburse would more than cover the cost of the person I needed to help me in addition to the boys' other needs. As it turned out, the reimbursement amount was rather generous. Had they shared that information with me earlier, the question of additional help would never have come up, because it was clear that it was a non-issue given the economics of it all.

However, that's not was happened. What I came away with was a very, very bad feeling about the high-handed way that DSS often deals with foster parents, some of whom are disenfranchised, marginalized people who want to do the right thing but who also rely heavily on the reimbursement they receive for being foster parents.

It occurred to me that I was not in the mold of most foster parents. In choosing to put me down, use the boys as pawns, and generally trample on everyone's rights, DSS was merely continuing a way of doing business established years before. Luckily, rationality prevailed in the person of the Area Director who removed the supervisor from the case, and restored order.

She should have been disciplined but never was. You can't expect too much. A solution was found after a tense meeting involving almost everyone in the case including someone from the state representative's office who had taken an interest in how one foster parent and three foster children were being treated.

I hardly saw this as a victory and was disappointed that there are still some people who would use kids, especially three like these, who had been poorly treated before. The experience solidified some of my impressions of DSS, but also enabled me to see that there were some in the organization who would do the right thing when called upon.

One person in DSS had created the problem but another one had found the solution. I resolved that I could put this aside and work for the kids' benefit but it also strengthened my desire to advocate for them. Victimized kids shouldn't continue to be victimized by those who are supposed to help them.

Only recently I have noted a shift in DSS's attitude toward dealing with foster parents when the inevitable crisis develops. In years past the foster parent and often the lowest-level caseworker would have been blamed. The bureaucrats would quickly have distanced themselves from both parent and staff member, and everyone would await the next crisis.

It's rare that a leader of a state child protective agency "owns" any of the problem, a problem that often develops because of poor supervision, monitoring, and unacceptably high caseload levels over which the foster parent and caseworker have no control. Now I see high-level DSS officials taking some share of responsibility when the causes of crises, including deaths of kids in foster care, are clearly systemic and organizational in nature. That's encouraging and many of us hope that it's a trend that will continue.

It must also be noted that the Commonwealth of Massachusetts made a huge financial commitment to this particular family in the form of residential and foster care placements. We are fortunate to live in a state that commits so much to children and families even if I think we can do more.

Things Begin to Unravel

In October, the first of the three brothers moved in, followed by the second in February, and the third in April. In each case the formal date of "move-in" was proceeded by a week or two of actually living in the house. All three were enrolled in the elementary school up the street from where our home was located.

The principal, a former school district special education director, welcomed the boys with open arms and the teachers were committed to working with them. Two of the three boys did remarkably well in public school. The third hated school and had a history of difficulty in class. Of the three he had the most difficulty because of a demonstrable language-based learning disability that translated into frustration, anger, and misbehavior. He also was in the class of a veteran teacher who was just about ready to retire and who wasn't particularly enthused about his disruptive, oppositional style.

All three brothers are engaging but each has his own style. The youngest brother charmed everyone in sight and was actually taken to the mother-son dance by his own second grade teacher. The fourth grader, the middle brother, a "mediator" in the true sense of that word, immediately made friends and was able to dispel images about former Perkins kids being "dorks" or "tards." Other kids liked him. He was athletic. He was as bright as they were, even if school wasn't his favorite thing. For the two youngest it was really a seamless re-integration back into public school. The oldest brother struggled.

At home they were doing well. We had the usual battles over homework from the oldest and the house menu from the youngest, a picky eater if there ever was one. Jay, the middle guy, thrived. He did his homework, continued to make friends, and ate like he was "going to the chair." It was only after a month or so that things began to surface – old conflicts, I think based on history – but not easy to surmount. The oldest and the youngest just didn't get along.

Before long that would make the whole arrangement unravel. I talked to a psychiatrist who I knew professionally and who had worked earlier with the boys. He made a point that is quite significant. Kids who are neglected, who are left for hours or days with no adult supervision, direction, care and love, often are more damaged than kids who suffer physical abuse (of course, for these, guys *both* had been alleged).

Physical abuse tends to be episodic. It happens. It stops. It happens again. However it isn't usually consistently present in the household. It can be contemporaneous with parental mood change, explosive incidents, or fueled by excessive alcohol use or drugs.

Neglect on the other hand is there and it's there all the time. It doesn't go away. Kids experience it all the time and over time it has deleterious effects that appear to overshadow the effects of periodic beatings and abuse. Interesting.

On one occasion when we returned to the eastern Massachusetts community where they had lived, they regaled me with stories. At virtually every corner, there was some event memorialized.

"Hey, remember when the cops pulled us off the roof of the Dunkin' Donuts?" "Remember when we caught the duck?" ("How?" you foolishly ask. Answer: "You put bread on the end of a hook, the same way you catch a fish!")

The middle brother told me that he had done community service when he and his older brother were found in an apartment that wasn't theirs. "A breaking and entering by a 6-year-old?" you ask incredulously. Yes, six and seven year olds can pull off a "B and E."

They all had "street smarts" galore, but the challenge especially for the oldest brother would be to learn to downplay those skills and to adapt to societal demands and expectations about behavior. Stealing will keep you alive on the street, but in a home setting rifling your foster father's change jar isn't a good idea. A smart mouth replete with every crude term possible helps to create the right street persona for self-protection purposes, but it doesn't play well in a suburban community and school.

At home there had been questions about their supervision and the local police and their teachers were quite concerned. The youngest guy spoke of how he was put in a garbage can and rolled down a hill as part of one of the "games" the neighborhood kids played. All three had an unusual number of injuries suggesting there was not enough adult supervision. Even now, one of them has some marks he just won't talk about. DSS intervened, moved them first into foster care and then into residential programs, but didn't move to terminate parental rights. That would prove to be a fateful decision, since the likelihood of adoption decreases for a child with each passing year.

There's also a fourth brother who I only met last year. He is similarly damaged and has been in a variety of residential programs for several years. Until recently the other three brothers had not seen him in seven or eight years. The reunion with them went well. Imagine not seeing your brother for seven years, from the time you were five years old until you turned 12! Amazing.

In some ways they are models of childhood resilience. To think someone could come back from that kind of history is truly amazing. However, they all have emerged as pretty well put together kids, although concerns remain about the behavior of one and the overall effects of the alleged sexual abuse on another. Time will tell, but the short-term assessment seems to be that things will work out for them. I have some real concerns about one of them who seems mired in his depression and who expresses anger in a variety of unhealthy ways.

I'm still not certain whether it was the history of neglect or some earlier interactions that made it impossible for them to live under the same roof. There were episodes of fire-setting, fondling the dog, and one pulling down his brother's pants, all of which signified that trouble lay ahead.

In the final analysis a decision had to be made that they would have to be separated and live in separate foster homes. Initially I felt a sense of defeat because I felt that I was responsible given the fact that I was a single parent.

Maybe if I had been able to supervise them constantly some of the incidents wouldn't have happened. I knew that was an unrealistic expectation however. I had to cook, take a shower, get dressed, and do a lot of other things that required me leaving them in another room of the house while I accomplished the task. When it became clear that I often couldn't do that, it was evident that we had a problem.

The youngest came back to Perkins before going off to another residential program in September 2003 and the oldest of the three went to a foster home about an hour and half away. Within a year and half they would all be re-united geographically when the oldest of the three returned to Perkins from foster care in July 2004, and the youngest, in February 2005, became the foster son of a staff member at Perkins.

Weekend visits with the fourth brother, who still lived in a residential program and whom the other three had only started seeing in the summer of 2005 after many years, were now part of the regular schedule. The oldest of the three who had lived with me got two more shots at foster care in late 2005 but those arrangements were short-lived. He ultimately was placed in a group home.

All four of the boys now see each other and visit with their mother regularly. The whole arrangement has had its ups and downs, but, right now, all of them are in less restrictive placements, an improvement from four years ago when they were all in residential treatment facilities. It has been encouraging to watch them grow and, in two cases, see them flourish in the community and in public school.

Residential Programs

I also had the opportunity to see how other residential programs operate as I visited two of the boys in their residential programs usually before taking them for an overnight or a weekend. The oldest brother had been in the same program for several years and lived in a beautiful house in a residential neighborhood in an area of Massachusetts known as Metrowest. The program was well run and the kids, all troubled teenagers, seemed to do well. It had a nice feel to it.

The youngest brother was placed in a residential program run by a large, reputable provider of child welfare services. It was located in an up and coming area of Boston but the facility itself was old and tired. What was worse was that the staff had no idea what they were doing, although they presented as "experts" in the field of children with hypersexualized behaviors. This last issue pervaded everything that happened in the program. The whole thing had a rather unhealthy feel to it.

From the beginning the program staff were adversarial toward me (a *former* foster parent) and to another visiting resource, a staff member at Perkins who had known the youngest brother from the day he came to Perkins. They tried to limit visits, discouraged overnights with his brother, and even attempted to halt holiday visits with the family.

Below is an edited version of a letter I sent to the CEO of the agency when a holiday visit was denied. I see no reason to embarrass the agency by identifying either the organization or the CEO. I was most gratified that I received a prompt response to the issues I raised. I include my letter so that the depth of my concern is evident.

Dear CEO:

I write to you as a fellow CEO of a child welfare agency in Massachusetts but also in the capacity of a former foster parent of a child currently in your care. I hope you'll listen to what I have to say.

I would classify this communication in the category of "what a CEO needs to know before it becomes embarrassing." I have been the recipient of such communications from time to time and, while I often dislike them initially, I later on appreciate them.

For the last 16 years I have been the Executive Director/CEO of the Doctor Franklin Perkins School in Lancaster, MA, an agency that serves children similar to those served by your organization, but which in addition runs programs for mentally retarded adults and seniors with special needs. Almost two years ago I began the process of, first, becoming a visiting resource and, then, a foster parent to three DSS-placed brothers who were going to be discharged separately from Perkins and who in all likelihood would have had very little contact in the future. While I had seen a number of heart-rending cases in the years I have been here, this was among the most compelling.

I became a foster parent to all three boys in the hope of keeping them together. They are the product of a home that you and I all too often encounter – one characterized by alleged drug abuse, domestic violence, physical and sexual abuse. As I recall, numerous 51-A's (complaints of abuse or neglect) were filed, many of which were substantiated. The kids – there were actually <u>four</u> boys - (I've never met the 4th) were routinely out on the streets - neglected, uncared for, involved with the police, etc., etc. At the time they were roughly 4, 5 and 7 years of age respectively. Hard to believe – but true.

My own two daughters had already graduated from college and moved away and the opportunity to make a difference in the lives of these three boys presented itself. I thought long and hard about this. Although I knew, as a single parent, that the obstacles were significant and that their histories were complicated, I applied to be a foster parent for the three of them. They were all together in my house for nearly four months having come in on a staggered schedule. At this writing I still have one of the boys with me (he has been with me for over a year); the other two have gone off to other placements. The possibility of them ever living together became less likely in the months that I actually had them living together in my home. The oldest of the three is in another foster home, the middle guy remains with me, and the youngest, now eight years old, is a resident in your program. And therein lies my tale of woe.

While your staff is very committed, they are also bound to a modality of treatment that I am not sure has achieved widespread acceptance. I am fearful that quasi-correctional and punitive elements have become part of a program philosophy. Reminiscent of the "strip them down to nothing and build them back up" thinking of the U.S. Marines, the philosophy seems to be to have kids stripped of all earlier relationships and then to start a process to build a relationship with a new foster family, totally devoid of earlier ties.

While this kind of thinking might work at Parris Island, (although I've never been convinced that it does) I question the efficacy when it is inflicted on already traumatized eight-year-olds. I am amazed at the regimentation, lack of sensitivity, and "cultish-like" adherence to untested principles of treatment. Children seem to be sacrificed to a philosophy that demands the creation of a whole new life by de-constructing all earlier relationships. It's really rather scary. It ill serves children.

My most recent encounter with the philosophy of the program was my request to have this boy spend Thanksgiving with his brother who lives with me. Initially we were told that, if the brother who lives with me was willing to engage in therapy at the program with his brother, and if a judgment could be made that the boys were "safe," then a visit for Thanksgiving would be "discussed." I was informed on Thursday that there would be no visit. No discussion. No debate. No visit.

The decision flew in the face of the earlier arrangement that was based on successful engagement in therapy and a judgment that the boys would be safe. Both of those conditions were fulfilled but the visit was denied. I'm still not sure how my foster son feels about the rug being slipped out from underneath him. Both boys were very sad and I'm certain this did nothing for the boy in your care's depression. A "pre-visit" that I was now told was also a pre-requisite of a holiday visit was never arranged by the program staff and now was being cited as an additional reason to deny the holiday visit - a rather disingenuous approach.

The primary reason given to me for denying the visit was some fear that a visit for Thanksgiving would "confuse" the young man who might think he would return to the home permanently. As I later explained to the staff, this boy is one of the most intellectually capable kids I have dealt with in the last twenty years. I felt that he had the capacity to both understand that he was not to come to my home permanently and was emotionally capable of arriving at that conclusion as well. I was amazed at how little they knew about this child. His mother has also not shown for her last two scheduled visits with him; he doesn't have too much going for him.

Suspecting that my own emotional involvement in the case was skewing my view of things, I asked members of the treatment team at my agency – a team which treated the same boy for three years – what their opinion was. It ranged from profound disbelief, to skepticism, to questions about "what are those people thinking about." In the time I have been involved in the administration of a residential facility, we have always made a special effort to get every kid out of here on holidays. While that entails careful analysis about danger and safety issues and sometimes results in a decision that a child should stay here, our bias is that they should leave here and experience a holiday in a "real home." The bias in your program is that the burden of proof is on the requesting significant other. The staff prefers kids *to stay in the institution* because of unfounded and groundless fears about potential "confusion." It's the difference between trying to have kids experience a positive warm celebration or being so guarded and so bound to an institutional philosophy that visits must be justified and defended. Very sad.

As of Friday afternoon, I received a call from the staff of the program which I viewed as the opening offer in some kind of bizarre bargaining session. I was told he could now come for Thanksgiving. A review had taken place, and the fears about confusion had now been allayed. When I began to discuss logistical issues of picking him up and returning him, there was a sudden change in the tone of the conversation. He was not being released for an overnight visit for Thanksgiving. If he was to come at all, it was to be a *day* visit – and a day visit *only*.

I was astounded – again. If the fears about "confusion" had been allayed, what now could be the issue? I must tell you that I fundamentally dislike negotiations over children because they inevitably are viewed as "pawns" in the process. I find that distasteful. I explained to the staff that logistically it was probably impossible given my daughters' traveling arrangements that I could manage a same day pick up and return.

We agreed to leave things as they were – there would be no visit. I felt to tell him that he might come, and then not be able to pick him up, would further exacerbate his already obvious sadness at the earlier decision to deny the visit. As of this writing I am still trying to figure out how to pull it all off. If there is any way to do it, I will.

I bring this to your attention because it falls into the category of "things a CEO should know." My agency is not as big as yours is but it operates in 22 buildings, at multiple sites in different towns, and we have a staff of 360 people. A CEO can't always know what's going on everywhere and all the time, but I find that it's nice to know things I otherwise wouldn't - even if I don't like hearing them initially.

I hope you don't like hearing this – and I hope you change some things over there. The staff may be well intentioned - but they ain't helping kids!

Best personal regards,
Charles P. Conroy, Ed.D.

Those of us who had worked so hard to keep these kids together were astonished at the recalcitrance and distaste for family exhibited by the program's staff, all accomplished ostensibly in the interest of "treatment." We weathered their incompetence and lack of diagnostic and treatment skills for a year and a half before the young man was discharged to that same visiting resource, now his foster mother.

She simply wouldn't give up when she was told that this kid had "too many people in his life." When I counted all the people in his life, I came up with his brothers, me, his visiting resource, and his mother. Too many people! That's patently ridiculous but the staff felt that their pronouncements should go unchallenged, even if they were outlandish.

The lesson I learned in this case was persistence. I fought them at every turn and continued to maintain that family was important and that their "treatment philosophy" did more damage than good. I continue to harbor major doubts about programs for kids who are labeled "sexual offenders" or "abuse-reactive" since my experience here was that a lot of what they do comes from "seat of the pants," "do as we tell you" thinking.

That attitude conceals the lack of an overall treatment framework or philosophy that has been tested in any fashion and found to be effective. I'm not sure that I'd characterize what they do as "snake oil," but I think the efficacy of their treatment needs to be analyzed much more than it has been. I got the feeling they often made it up as they went along.

When he was finally discharged, we were all relieved. In the time since that happened he has done remarkably well. Contrary to the predictions of the staff in this program, he has integrated well into community life and is a great success in school. The predictions of dire sexualized behavior have not only not materialized but we have seen that normalization and someone in his life who is totally committed to him have made all the difference in the world. The staff of that program was uniformly wrong. It's that simple.

For me, I came to understand how important it is for residential programs to work closely with families and significant people in the lives of kids. Parents, foster parents, and people who know kids in treatment do have much to offer. To ignore them totally or veto their suggestions because the "treatment philosophy" is paramount is simply a bad way of working with people. High-handed, exclusionary treatment practices don't work for kids who need to maintain the bond of family and connection with significant others. I've tried to bring that back to Perkins when I occasionally notice professionals who denigrate the opinions of people who are "*just* parents."

"Little Things"

One of the key things I have learned is how important the home environment is for kids who have been in residential treatment. I have found that they love the "little things" about living in a home rather than a "program," as kids refer to treatment facilities.

When the oldest of the four brothers first started his weekend visits, I continued the practice of cooking big weekend meals. The first time he came I bought New York strip steaks from our favorite butcher. He wolfed it all down along with copious amounts of French fries, salad, and corn. Later on, his younger brother confided in me that the oldest brother had said to him, "That's the best meal I ever had."

We try to do the best we can in residential treatment programs and to prepare the best food possible. However there's something about a steak grilled outside and eaten with your brother with no one else a part of the meal that makes it taste better. (That, and my excellent culinary skills!)

On Sundays especially I always made sure there was a roast in the oven. Because I had the time, we always had mashed potatoes too - not the flakes from a box, but the real thing. The smell of roast beef, pot roast, or loin of pork lends a certain feeling to a home on a Sunday afternoon in autumn or winter. I was amazed almost from the beginning how much they liked just being in a room warmed by a fireplace or eating homemade cookies or cakes, which they loved to help prepare. Little things. They make all the difference.

As of this writing, all is as well as can be expected. All four brothers are in better shape than in all the time I've known them. Jay recently took a commuter train by himself to have lunch with his mother in their hometown. Now, that's encouraging.

What Kids Need

From time to time I have had my differences with the Department of Social Services. However, in this case, (and with the exception of the little contretemps we had at the initiation of the foster care arrangement) I think the Department has been magnificent.

The commitment to this family and especially to keeping siblings in close contact has been wonderful. The resources of time and money have been substantial but are beginning to pay dividends. Two of the brothers are definitely college material and, in Massachusetts, should they choose, they can attend the state university or one of the state colleges tuition-free. That's quite a bonus and a nice way to cap a history in foster care. There's talk right now of extending more DSS services to kids through age 21 and that would be extraordinary.

We struggle in residential treatment and foster care to put kids on the right track and keep them there and to make them successful, productive, law-abiding citizens. Commitment through age 21 can only help.

Let's face it. We don't expect that our own kids will be self-sufficient before 21, so how can we have higher expectations for kids in care? There's a very obvious trend right now of coming home from college to live with Mom and Dad for a few more years before going out on one's own. So, how can we expect more from kids in care than our own kids?

My own odyssey is probably somewhat different than a lot of foster parents because of what I do professionally. I firmly believe there is a useful and necessary role for residential programs and I think some small proportion of kids will always need such programs. However, there is also dire need for good, committed foster parents who are willing to work with kids who have special challenges and often incredibly painful histories. We also desperately need people to adopt.

We need adults to come forward to provide warm, nurturing homes for kids who often have never known a healthy relationship with a parental figure. These kids need a home environment that is inviting and enjoyable but which has also rules, stability, and continuity. The last three are the hallmarks for success but they are secondary to love and nurturance and an ability to help kids through life's difficulties.

2001-2002

Terrorist Attacks "Unfathomable"
(Reprinted from *The Item*, Clinton, MA September 2001)

She could never say it right. As a three-year-old, it was always the World *Train* Center. Maybe kids relate a lot more easily to trains than commerce. I corrected it a few times before I realized I was licked and then I called it the same thing. By the time she had turned 10 or so, it was one of those inside family things that had worn thin but which fathers just won't let die.

Last Tuesday, I was on the phone with that same young lady, now 21, and a confirmed New Yorker, despite having moved with her family to Lancaster almost fifteen years before. As we were talking about the planes, which only moments before had intentionally plowed into the buildings, the first tower collapsed. She drew her breath, dissolved into tears, and could barely whisper the words into the phone. "It's gone," she gasped, shortly to be followed by its twin. Gone.

Despite my initial objections and concerns about safety, the product of my living in that metropolis for 38 years, she decided to attend college in New York City. It's tough to argue against your own alma mater and that's the university she had chosen. I never had a chance. She went and she loved it.

We talked as so many other parents did on Tuesday about the horrific scene before our eyes. But this was a special conversation. There was simply too much history here. I had spent untold hours at the World Trade Center negotiating teacher contracts, first as a union official and later as management.

I remember being in Two World Trade Center, the south tower, when the lights went out one night. The lights went out every night unless you let the front desk know you were staying late. There were no light switches on the walls; it was all done by computer and all centralized just like the high-speed elevators that departed and arrived on a predetermined schedule. I recall how eerie it was late at night and some nights we were there near midnight. The building creaked, we were told, because they had some "sway" built into them to accommodate the high winds at such heights. Memories.

When the girls were young and the tourists weren't around, we did the Staten Island Ferry, World Trade Center, and Statue of Liberty "thing." We marveled at how far you could see into New Jersey and Pennsylvania from 110 stories up. We weren't part of the elegant Windows on the World set, and only managed to knock down hot dogs, popcorn, and soda way up in the sky. More memories - nice memories.

The towers (until last Tuesday) were magnificent structures where tens of thousands came to work every day. They altered, for about thirty years, the entire skyline of the city. I think they had their own zip code. The Empire State Building of my parents' generation, the structure on which King Kong perched years before, had seen its heyday when the towers were opened in the early 70's. They symbolized New York and the supremacy of American commerce and engineering prowess. They also helped young families create indelible memories.

Two days after I spoke to the New York daughter, I phoned my brother who only recently retired as a police officer for the Port Authority, the owner, operator and landlord of the towers. He figured he knew 30 guys buried in the rubble. We only speculated how many of the hundreds of firemen either of us might know. Until then, thankfully, we hadn't heard any familiar names. John McLoughlin, a fellow cop, according to a story making the rounds and later confirmed by the *New York Times*, had been removed from the rubble with two broken legs. He was on the 82nd floor when the tower collapsed! Doesn't sound possible.

He's just one of the thousands of stories we'll hear in the days to come of those immolated when tons of airplane fuel were dumped on them, those buried for eternity beneath the wreckage and twisted steel, or splattered red on the sidewalk below. It's unfathomable.

Later, on Tuesday as dusk began to encircle central Massachusetts, I passed by one of the bedrooms in the house and I was struck by a bit of irony. On the wall of this room is a huge panorama about four feet long. It's a picture of lower Manhattan at night with the Brooklyn Bridge at the lower right and the two huge towers that transformed the world's view of Manhattan at the upper left. The picture is in the room of the young woman who rarely slept there anymore, the confirmed New Yorker, the same young woman who only hours before had wept when she saw the first one crumble.

The World *Train* Center is gone but our fond memories of it are very much alive. More importantly, as I view that picture, which I have since moved to a more prominent place, I wonder if the loss of those structures is only the beginning of something so huge, so profoundly horrific, that I should even try to contemplate it.

At a pivotal point in the Second World War Winston Churchill said, "This is not the end. It's not even the beginning of the end - but it's probably the end of the beginning." We have yet to come that far. A week after the towers collapsed, we haven't even seen the end of the beginning. What more memories will be made?

A Christmas Foster Care Story
Scene: The Bethlehem Office of DSS
Case: Christ, Jesus. DOB: 12/25/00

"You two got picked up by the cops last night in a stable with a two-day old baby and a donkey which apparently serves as your primary mode of transportation," intoned the DSS case manager.

"That's right sir," answered the shy young lady who looked to be about 16 years old.

"And the cops said that this guy over here isn't the baby's father," continued the DSS worker. "Apparently you had some kind of "encounter" with an angel, you were "overshadowed," - if I have the term correct - and now you got this kid. Jesus!"

"That's right," says the young girl, "Jesus."

"So you and the baby have had zero pre-natal care – no sonogram, no amnio – nuttin'? You probably ain't seen a folic acid capsule in nine months either – right, honey?"

"That's true," says the girl.

"Sweetie, I gotta tell ya," says the DSS man, "ya ain't making this easy. I think I gotta go 51A here, maybe move for a C&P, and get you three some help. Joey here says he's the foster father but he's not on the approved list. He hasn't attended one training. He doesn't know a thing about child development, family dynamics, community-based, MAP, CPR - nothing!"

"I'm a carpenter," says Joseph.

"Yeah, I know, Joey. And if you spent a little more time with your tool box and a little less time "overshadowing" young ladies, we wouldn't be doin' this, knucklehead. I'll handle this, lover boy. Then we'll get to why a guy your age is hanging with a 16-year-old babe and a two-day-old kid. Where I come from they call that statutory…"

"The girl got in trouble and I helped her out," says Joseph. "I ain't no saint. Well, actually... You think I wanted to haul ass - literally - from Nazareth to this dump and then have to deal with the cops and DSS, you moron? Why don't you pucker up and plant one on the donkey over there!"

"Hey, Joey, Joey baby - let's get one thing straight. I'm DSS. *We* don't kiss ass - people kiss *ours*!

Case notes many years later

The early prognosis in this case was not good - a mother who wouldn't own her own risk-taking behavior and who consistently maintained that she had miraculous encounters with an angel and the Almighty that resulted in her pregnancy. Her visual hallucinations didn't recur over the years and she seemed to do remarkably well despite the strains and tensions of motherhood.

The couple had exercised incredibly poor judgment in traveling such a huge distance, not making arrangements for lodging beforehand, and generally not planning a single aspect of what, thankfully, was an uneventful pregnancy. It is amazing that this tenuous relationship could be sustained for any reasonable length of time.

The outlook for this child, a seven-pound male at birth, was not good although this single Mom and her *ad hoc* foster care "support" were clearly committed to the child. In his youth and adolescence the child did fairly well and the family was supervised by the Nazareth area office of DSS. When bullied or annoyed by others, the child, Jesus, ignored his taunters and inevitably responded that he had "*invisible* means of support."

Never a truly competent carpenter like his foster father, Jesus nonetheless was able to hammer an occasional nail and pretty much stayed out of trouble. He often spent time talking to elders, precociously discussing the pressing events of the day. When his parents tried to "re-focus" him, he was adamant that he was doing "his father's business" – whatever that meant.

Not a particularly recalcitrant, aggressive, or difficult child by nature, Jesus always seemed to be "on a mission." He didn't care what others thought of that. Early on, Oppositional Defiant Disorder was a distinct diagnostic possibility, although the professionals ultimately settled on ADHD. He consistently daydreamed, rarely stayed on task, and generally "did his own thing."

A mixture of nurture, nature and a little Ritalin was the key to success in this case. A single mom who really cared, good foster care, family support, stability, and consistency, combined with genetics on his bio father's side (which was nothing short of divine!) all helped.

Jesus had an excellent physical constitution, was rarely sick, and had a unique ability to heal quickly, something he readily shared with others. When he needed some help with his diagnosed attention deficits and hyperactivity, the farsighted Nazareth School Committee approved his attendance for one year at a specialized day treatment program. He did well.

Additional Commentary

On one of his first ventures into the larger social world as an adult, he was confronted at a wedding reception by an embarrassed host who had seen the wine supply quickly depleted. When his mother (that frightened 16-year-old of long ago who gave birth in a stable) noticed the predicament, she ordered the headwaiter to listen carefully to what Mr. Christ might say. Jesus whispered something in the waiter's ear. Soon after, the place was awash in the finest Chardonnay.

Mary asked the waiter what Jesus had said to him. He quizzically responded, "he looked me straight in the eye and said:

"A funny song. A funny dance.

A little seltzer down your pants.

> I'll help the host and his daughter.
> Just put out big jars of water.
> It's not your problem. It's really mine.
> Now go check out the five-star wine!"

The guests were truly amazed. Those who were still ambulatory came up to Jesus and slurred their profound gratitude for providing the highlight of the Cana social season – indeed, the *only* event of the Cana social season. Jesus' response was to allude to his humble beginnings in supervised foster care.

In response to the guests' incessantly shouted thank yous, and, as he rode off on his trusted colt, he roared, "Vino from tap water! Not too shabby for a guy who grew up in a house where the booze and meds were locked up – eh?"

Another success! Overcoming the odds. It's what we help kids do. Go foster care!

Merry Christmas and a happy new year.

Commencement Address
Anna Maria College
Paxton MA
May 19, 2002

His Excellency Bishop Reilly, reverend clergy, members of religious orders, trustees of the college, devoted Sisters of St. Anne, President McGarry, esteemed faculty, dedicated alumni, distinguished representatives of sister institutions of higher education, long-suffering and soon to-be-relieved parents, accomplished members of the Class of 2002 of Anna Maria College - friends all:

Commencement speeches and - I'm sorry to say many commencement speakers - are seldom memorable. When I spoke a few weeks back with President McGarry, I mentioned to him that of all the graduations I have ever attended – my own, my children's and many others - there are very few speakers I can even remember. I can recall even fewer of their messages.

The one that does stand out in my memory is my own college graduation - but it stands out for the wrong reason. Halfway through Daniel Patrick Moynihan's address to my Fordham University class, a large number of the undergraduates in 1970 got up and walked out to protest. In his position as Counselor to President Nixon he was correctly or incorrectly associated with the invasion of Cambodia during the conflict in Southeast Asia. So - that's pretty scary when you think about it. The only address I remember of all those ancient graduations speeches is the one where the audience, and indeed the most crucial part of the audience, got up and walked out.

Don't anybody move!

A lot of what I've learned over the years has come from my association these last thirty years with a variety of interesting kids. Kids have a certain penetrating wisdom about them. I recently came across two pieces that serve as great advice to speakers on occasions like this. Both were written by kids and were responses to classroom assignments to write short biographies of historical figures. One kid picked Socrates and the other selected Julius Caesar.

The biography of Socrates read succinctly:
"Socrates was a great philosopher.
He went around giving people advice.
They poisoned him."

Of Julius Caesar another student wrote:
"Caesar was a great Roman general.
He gave very long speeches.
They killed him."

I don't want to be treated like Moynihan and I certainly don't want to get what Socrates and Caesar got. I hope you'll stay seated for the next few minutes. I'll go easy on dispensing advice, so you don't mistake me for Socrates – and - I won't be too long winded, so you don't think I'm Caesar. That way you get to hear the message and I get out of here alive.

On an occasion like this, I could easily launch into a recitation of events that occurred during your educational careers to help put things in historical perspective. I could mention that in the years 1980 or 1981, the years when most of you graduating seniors were born, many memorable events occurred. In 1980, Ronald Reagan was elected President, Beatle John Lennon was killed outside the Dakota apartments on the West Side of Manhattan, and the Soviet Union invaded Afghanistan, something the U.S. would do 21 years later.

In 1981, Reagan and the Pope would both be the victims of assassination attempts. Prince Charles and Lady Diana Spencer were married and Sandra Day O'Connor joined the United States Supreme Court becoming the first woman associate justice in our history. When many of you were in kindergarten or first grade, the Challenger exploded killing Christa McAuliffe, a teacher, and all her fellow astronauts. There was a major nuclear accident at a place called Chernobyl in what we then called the Soviet Union.

William Shroeder died after living over 600 days as the world's second artificial heart recipient. Death camp survivor, Elie Wiesel, was the recipient of the Nobel Peace Prize. The previous year he had been awarded an honorary degree from Anna Maria College. You were five or six years old. Other events that occurred during your high school and college careers that may be seared in your memory are more recent tragedies like the Oklahoma City bombing and the Columbine high school shootings.

One event more dramatic than all the earlier tragedies occurred at the very outset of your senior year here at Anna Maria College. You will long remember where you were on this campus and maybe even in what class you were when you heard of the destruction of the World Trade Center Towers in New York City, the almost simultaneous attempted annihilation of the Pentagon, and the crash in Pennsylvania of an airliner, all orchestrated by terrorists seeking to forever alter the American psyche, spirit and way of life. For the first time in your life, my life, and the lives of every American alive, our own air space was violated and mass destruction accomplished in our own homeland, a prospect once thought impossible.

That trauma and uncertainty about the world in which we live has since been compounded by uncertainties in our business and corporate community, notably the Enron fiasco and the complicity of one of America's most admired accounting firms, and the earlier failure of other American businesses previously thought invulnerable to the vagaries of a sagging economy.

More recently we have seen a challenge to the Catholic Church that is rivaled in its potential for division and destruction only by the reformation of Martin Luther and Henry VIII nearly five hundred years ago. The reverberations from the scandal, which had its beginnings in Boston, continue to dominate the headlines and jar our sensibilities almost daily.

What a year this has been!

To be finishing college when all that is going on makes it even more unsettling than usual to be embarking on a new career and a new phase of life in a world that seems so very different than what it was even twelve short months ago.

One wonders: is our world crumbling? Are there any constants? Where will it all end? When will it end? Will we see peace and stability in our country, in our business community and economic system, and in our church in our lifetimes? Have we been relegated to lives of perpetual turmoil and a constant struggle with the unknown. Are there any answers? Is anything left to hold on to?

The Irish poet William Butler Yeats in his poem *The Second Coming* sets the stage and describes a world that is eerily similar to what we've experienced.

Yeats says:
> Turning and turning in the widening gyre
> The falcon cannot hear the falconer;
> Things fall apart; the center cannot hold;
> Mere anarchy is loosed upon the world,
> The blood-dimmed tide is loosed, and everywhere
> The ceremony of innocence is drowned;
> The best lack all conviction, while the worst
> Are full of passionate intensity.

Let me say that again: "The best lack all conviction and the worst are full of passionate intensity." I'm not certain that Yeats is right but, if he is, our task is to reverse that. Our country, our economic and social systems (including the American family and our church) must become the focus of our passionate intensity. I'm not prepared to say that we lack conviction about all or any of them but it's clear that, if we believe in them, we must be prepared to defend them, take charge of them, and where needed, change them.

So much of that will fall to your generation rather than mine since these issues are not ones that can be addressed and resolved overnight. It is much more likely that we are looking at long-term intergenerational solutions than "quick fixes" to our current problems.

<u>You</u> will end up dealing with the problems of terrorism, the problems and inequities of the American economic system, the resurgence of the American family and the reformation of a wounded and hurting church. <u>You</u> will end up doing it when you take your rightful and inevitable

leadership roles in government, society, as parents, and as increasingly empowered lay leaders of a clergy-depleted church. You will confront all these issues because you know the good of the wider world depends on more than personal accomplishment. It means improving life generally – not just improving your own circumstances.

The solutions to the problems of world peace, stabilization of world economics, honesty in business, and creating religious institutions reflective of the needs of the people they serve will go well beyond your generation to the next. I also believe that it is in your role as parents that you will do your most effective work and make your most lasting contribution since the solutions to these problems will go well beyond your generation to the next.

While this is probably a role you don't contemplate too often in your life at this time, it will be a crucial one as time goes on. Your ability to raise a generation of decent, honest, law-abiding, equity-minded, citizens will be your ultimate task and the criteria on which you will be judged. The problems will continue and will need to be addressed over the long-term because they developed over the long term.

Some years ago management expert Peter Senge of MIT reminded us of the Parable of the Boiled Frog. With my apologies to the animal rights advocates among us, I beg your indulgence because it is just that - a parable. If you take a frog and put him into a pot of boiling water, he will jump out. However, if you place a frog in a pot of warm water and gradually turn up the heat the result is quite different. In the latter experiment, the frog becomes soporific, then comatose, and ultimately is boiled to death.

The lesson is clear. Our demise rarely comes because of quick, unpredictable and cataclysmic events. Most things that truly threaten us took years to develop. Terrorism didn't start with those planes slamming into the buildings in lower Manhattan; dishonesty may have culminated in the Enron tragedy but it certainly didn't start there; and our Church's current problems didn't begin in Boston - and they didn't begin in January.

It is time to re-embrace truth, family, honesty and God. It is time to prepare ourselves to raise a new generation of children who can face what we have left them and to resolve the problems of that troubled legacy.

When I met a few weeks back with several of your senior classmates here at the college I was struck by the fact that amid all the upsetment, instability, and challenges to our way of life, they found this place to be something of an oasis – an oasis - not a refuge. While this campus is safe, they didn't feel insulated from the outside world. Rather, they felt that the stability here better enabled them to deal with the tragic events of our ever-changing, unstable world.

They noted that among the graduating seniors you have been spared deaths and tragedies among the class. However, you were quite aware of the losses of others in the tragic national events I have pointed to as well as the horrible Worcester Cold Storage fire in December 1999. In many ways the caring faculty, the small class size, and the friendly, collegial atmosphere of this campus prepared you to face the tragedies and events of recent years and months. Those challenges will continue beyond today and we all fervently wish you will persevere and face them as you have already.

A few months ago I read a troubling piece by a Boston Globe columnist. She recounted how a kid in her Catholic religious education class, after a discussion focusing on Christ's emphasis on humility and forgiveness, made an observation. He flipply opined, "what a loser!"

Can you imagine! Whether you're a Christian or not – that kid's opinion should set you off - not just because of the personalized disrespect but also because of what that kid is saying in the larger sense. The values of humility and forgiveness and respect for others transcend Christianity. Devout Moslems, Buddhists, Jews and virtually all other systems of religion place value on our relationship with our fellow human beings. Even committed atheists would acknowledge human dignity and the value of service to others.

Even if it's not exactly framed as "love your neighbor as you love yourself," it's embedded in the teachings of the world's great religions. Senator Hubert Humphrey moved it into the political arena when he said that "the test of government is how we treat those in the dawn of life, the children; those in the twilight of life, the elderly; and those in the shadows of life, the disabled and disenfranchised."

That kid in the religious ed class just didn't see it. Maybe he didn't see it because he was just being a wise guy middle schooler (and I hope that's the easy explanation) but maybe he couldn't see it because he truly believes those things are not important. We have to tell him and the kids of the next generation – your children - that those things are indeed important. How you treat other people is crucial and is the ultimate test for all of us. The vision statement of the college underscores the need to offer service to others. You've heard it and you are prepared.

That loser to whom this misguided kid refers spent a good deal of his time with society's outcasts. Mary Magdalene, as I recall, was a practitioner of the world's oldest profession. The same is true of the woman this "loser" ran into and stopped from being stoned by the more righteous. The guy he looked over at on the adjacent cross was a common thief, a punk. They say he was a *good* thief, and I cynically inquire, if he was so good, why was he hanging on a cross. He may have been a good and contrite man but he was a lousy thief. Good thieves don't get caught! Ask the guys at Enron!

Remember what our "loser" friend said to the thief on the next cross? "This day you will be with me in paradise." Who else do you know who got such an ironclad guarantee? There's a lot of people we can surmise found Paradise as their final destination, but it was the wise-guy, two-bit thief hanging on the cross who got the guarantee without any fine print. Not bad. A loser who was hanging out (literally) with another "loser."

Maybe the world needs more "losers" – or maybe we just need people to convince the next generation - your children - that taking care of others, providing loving and caring service, being humble about it, and forgiving the transgressions of others doesn't make you a loser. It makes you a winner. Let's tell them that. <u>You</u> tell them that. You'll be the parents soon and you have to tell them and you have to model the way.

I make it sound much too easy, much too principled, and much too black and white, and it's not. It never has been. Doing things that are right can often bring the scorn of others who simply don't understand or who just disagree with what you're doing.

Is our world crumbling? Is Christ a loser? Can we go on the way we are? <u>You</u> decide because, more and more, it's getting to be your problem and it will be <u>your</u> decisions in the final analysis that will make the difference.

This college has given you the opportunity and the value system within which to make decisions without making them for you and that's what we are all faced with in life. The test for each of us is how we respond and how well we teach our children to respond. As your classmates were able to point out to me, this college to which you say farewell today, has clearly assisted you in formulating your response and by extension the response of your children's generation to the political, economic, religious and family problems we will continue to face.

Last year at my daughter's graduation Bill Cosby offered his advice and noted that there are many different kinds of graduates. Some graduate cum laude, others magna cum laude, still others summa cum laude – and then there's a fourth category – "oh thank you, Lordy!" Regardless of where you fall in that hierarchy – this is your day. You deserve it because of your hard work and your parents deserve it because of their hard work.

This is only the beginning. The challenges in this rapidly changing world continue to expand. Your role in it from this minute on has expanded. What you do and what you teach your children to do will ensure that our way of life is sustained and improved.

We trust in you and know you will succeed. As we offer our congratulations on this wonderful day, we express our heartfelt confidence that you will succeed.

Today there should be a sense of accomplishment and I hope a sense of relief; satisfaction in achieving a goal and completing a job well done; and a little bit of "oh, thank you, Lordy" as well.

Congratulations.

"Yuh-huh"
Perkins School Recognition Day
June 15, 2002

There's a guy in modern literature who has mastered the art of the brief welcome. In the first Harry Potter book, which came out as a film this past year, Albus Dumbledore, Headmaster of Hogwarts, welcomed the students at the beginning of the term.

Remember his greeting? "Welcome to a new year at Hogwarts! Before we begin, I would like to say a few words. And here they are: Nitwit! Blubber! Oddment! Tweak! Thank you."

Four words and then he sat down. That's the way to welcome people – *short and sweet*.

You're in no such luck this morning.

I can't avoid noting that this is a school year that started with the most horrific single day in all of our lifetimes. 9/11 is seared into our memories and has changed our lives. However if there's one thing we've learned, it's that life goes on. Despite what happened nine months ago this has still been a year of personal growth, academic advancement, and if you look across the lawn, great expansion.

I have been reminded continually of how much growth there has been because of a closer association I've had with three young brothers at the Pappas Home whom I have come to know much better in the last few months. As a result I've learned a lot as I have watched them learn. As all of you, they have grown physically, academically, athletically, and socially. They are bright, funny, and talented and you can actually see growth day by day and week by week.

I often see things from a different perspective now. I've watched an eight-year-old gasp as he watched a great blue heron soar from a rock in the middle of a silent lake late on a Friday afternoon. I've seen his older brother snare a turtle with his bare hand after I told him there was no way he'd get close enough to grab one. He did it three times and had the good sense not to say "I told you so" to someone who can't stand to hear "I told you so." I have seen the seven-year-old master his gymnastics skills including pulling off a perfect but unscheduled headstand on third base during a baseball game on the Manor lawn.

That same guy couldn't resist jumping in the lake on one of those 90-degree days in April only to find himself with a wet tee shirt and the need for a dry one as the wind picked up. As I went through folded piles of adult-size tees shirts his frustration mounted. When all I could offer was an oversized sweatshirt, he slowly intoned, "Don't you have any *little* clothes!"

We've seen sparrow eggs become sparrow chicks. We've journeyed to the island in the lake to see that the Canada goose had all along been sitting on eggs that were almost the size of baseballs. We knew we would soon be treated to a new goose family swimming the lake. I was able to see what a lot of the staff sees here all the time – growth, eagerness to learn, reasonable risk-taking, and satisfaction with one's accomplishments. This year I learned a lot too.

After a 10-year self-imposed exile from McDonald's, I now know what a McFlurry is as well as the contents of a happy meal - two things I'm relatively certain I could have gotten happily through life without knowing - but which have expanded my horizons as well as my waist. My classical radio station less frequently is played in the car and as a result, I now know all the words to "Won't You Be My Girlfriend." By the way those are all the words to "Won't You Be My Girlfriend."

We know that, while it may be okay to eat with your hands at McDonald's because there's no alternative – it's not acceptable at a nice restaurant where they provide you with utensils, specifically a fork. When I raised that issue, I again had my vocabulary enriched.

I said, "the waiter gave you a fork with your lunch. You should use it."

His response was, "they're French fries. You don't need a fork."

"This isn't McDonald's," I went on. "You can pick up the hamburger but the fries get eaten with a fork."

The next response is one I have since heard many times. To my repeated suggestion that he eat with a fork, he signified his disagreement by a slight shaking of his head and uttering, "nuh-huh." Being significantly more mature and articulate, my response was a terse, "yuh-huh."

Those words have gradually made their way into my vocabulary. I'm deathly afraid it will come out at the wrong time. What happens, if at the Board meeting next week, I am asked about the financial prospects for next year by an astute Trustee?

"Charlie," he might ask, "with the state situation as it is, aren't you fearful that we will run a deficit next year?"

"Nuh-huh," I'm afraid I'll answer.

To the question, "Are you sure we will be able to open the new building on time," I might just volunteer, "Yuh-huh."

I have found it exciting to see them grow. They're only three examples of what has gone on across this campus, every day, and all year long for all of you. That's what we celebrate today – your growth, your learning, your maturity, and your ability to collaborate, cooperate and get along with others. It has been a wonderful school year despite the rocky start of 9/11. That day will long be remembered but it has not stopped us from living, growing, and being hopeful about what's to come.

Has this been a great year?"
"Yuh-huh!"
"Have we done all we can do and gone as far as we can go?"
"Nuh-huh!"

I return to where I began – to Harry Potter - and conclude with the words of the Hogwarts School song. What it lacks in poetic flair it makes up for in an uplifting statement of perseverance, cooperative learning, and a belief that education is for all of us at all ages.

> Hogwarts, Hogwarts, Hoggy Warty Hogwarts,
> Teach us something please,
> Whether we be old and bald
> Or young with scabby knees.
>
> Our heads could do with filling
> With some interesting stuff,
> For now they're bare and full of air,
> Dead flies and bits of fluff.
>
> So teach us things worth knowing
> Bring back what we've forgot,
> Just do your best, we'll do the rest,
> And learn 'til our brains all rot.

To which I add a hearty, "yuh-huh."

"Sleep with the Light On"
Perkins Staff Awards Dinner
August 22, 2002
Manor Lawn

There's a story I heard a long time go about President Harry Truman that underscores well the need to speak in language that is unambiguous, maybe even blunt, when one is discussing matters so important and so grave that they require straight talk to get to the heart of the matter. Truman was giving a speech in the Midwest as I recall and he went on and on using the kind of blunt language he was known for. His wife, Bess, was in the audience and was seated with a local woman, a pillar of the community, who heard Truman's message but was appalled at his earthy language.

At the conclusion of Truman's talk, the woman turned to Mrs. Truman and said, "I like what Harry has to say but he didn't have to say the word, 'manure,' so many times."

Bess Truman looked at the woman and responded, "Actually it's an improvement. It took me 20 years to get him to say 'manure.'"

It's time to talk in blunt terms about a current issue, maybe one we have all had quite enough of frankly, but one which needs to be discussed. The issue of course is abuse – child abuse – and more specifically child sexual abuse. It's among the most distasteful topics one can bring up, but unfortunately circumstances over the course of the last year demand that we as an organization make our position crystal clear on the topic.

Our role at Perkins transcends the provision of education and residential treatment for children and adults with special needs. Although maybe not quite conscious of it every day, we must also be advocates of certain positions and philosophies that will improve the lives and in some cases heal the wounds of the children we serve. While we privately advocate for children, we must also *publicly* advocate for them as well. We as an organization are sworn to serve, treat, educate and help kids with unique needs and special histories and we can't be indifferent when it comes to articulating what is in their interest.

Elie Wiesel, the Nobel Peace Prize winner and survivor of the Holocaust, spoke about the perils of indifference at a White House symposium in 1999. He said:

"Indifference can be tempting - more than that, seductive. It is so much easier to look away from victims.

He went on:

"Indifference is...a strange and unnatural state in which the
lines blur between light and darkness, dusk and dawn, crime
and punishment, cruelty and compassion, good and evil."

None of us individually is indifferent when it comes to the discussion of sexual abuse of children but I am talking about the organization's response. We see the results of mistreatment and abuse all the time. We see the children who behave poorly and who are ostracized because they are reliving earlier experiences of horrible mistreatment. They do things that are unpleasant or even antisocial and very few people scrape the surface and look for the reasons why they do those things. Some, having scraped the surface, don't like what they see, deny the reality of it, and choose to put these children out of sight and out of mind. Their response is one of indifference.

As an organization serving children, many who have been the victims of sexual abuse, our response must be a vigorous, well-articulated position that sexual abuse of children under any circumstances by an adult is morally reprehensible, indefensible, and should be met with society's scorn and criminal and civil legal responses for the perpetrators.

I have always been struck by how, even after their victimization, some of these kids can still remain kids at heart. Some can't, but many do. At their core, even though they have been through things you and I never will, they remain children who are somehow able to go about their childhoods in simple ways, although they often have episodes where their history comes back to haunt them and where it is evident in periodic behavioral deterioration.

I had occasion to view this a while ago, when one of the young kids from Perkins was with me and was stung by a yellow jacket. If it's ever happened to you, you know that a yellow jacket sting is startling and intense but not particularly long-lasting presuming you are not allergic. When this eight-year-old was stung, he cried out immediately, quickly ran inside, and threw himself on the couch, face down, crying.

I told him that it was a yellow jacket sting, that I would put ice on it, and the pain would go away in ten minutes. The tears were streaming down his face as I tried to console him and he looked at me and expressed his disbelief that such an unprovoked attack could ever occur. He certainly hadn't done anything to justify this. With his wonderful little speech irregularity, he blurted out, "how could a animal be dat cruel?"

He happens to be one of the nicest, sweetest, most even-tempered kids I've ever met and his response to this little crisis in his life is indicative of how he views things and I think people generally. He pretty much likes and gets along well with every human being with whom he comes in contact. When he was being counseled recently by his older brother about who might be excluded from his birthday party, his answer was, "But how can I do that. Won't they be sad?"

Despite his history of neglect and abuse, he retains a capacity for empathy and compassion that surpasses that of almost any person you are likely to meet. He is a victim but one who is still connected to other people and who thinks of himself in terms of others and how he affects others. He's a wonderful kid as so many of our kids are. We as an organization must validate their hurt and enunciate our view that the abuse they have experienced is intolerable and must never be perpetrated again on any other children. Maybe that's quite a feat and maybe it's an unachievable goal or unattainable objective - but it's one that we must pursue.

Several years ago I used Lorenzo Carcaterra's book, *Sleepers*, to illustrate some points about abuse. The book was later turned into a movie starring Robert DeNiro as a Catholic priest who lies on the stand in a criminal trial to protect three men, mistreated and sexually abused as children, who have murdered one of the perpetrators of that abuse. Surfing channels, I recently found that the movie was on and I began to watch it. One of the exchanges in the movie got my attention. I guess I missed it when I read it the first time.

The plot to get the two murderers a "not guilty" verdict is being hatched by two friends, both childhood buddies of the alleged murderers and also victims of the same abuse by the same abusers. One, a district attorney who plans to purposely "lose" the case in order to get his friends off, is trying to convince his other buddy, a journalist, to help get some information and to get the priest on board with the scheme. When the journalist momentarily balks, the district attorney, his childhood friend, reminds him of the sexual abuse they all underwent as kids.

"Do you still sleep with the light on?" he asks him.

There's silence. The answer is clear.

The younger brother of the little boy who was stung by the bee is also a frequent visitor to my home. The first time he stayed overnight with his two brothers, he asked that a light be left on. I later went out and got a nightlight because the larger light disturbs the sleep of his brother roommate. We've been able over time to limit the light to virtually nothing, but this made a point. Always the need to have some light. Always the need to be guarded. Always the need to be aware that someone might tip toe into your room at night and do unspeakable things to you because that's what people did to you in the past. Seven years old and full of such worries! I read an assessment of this little guy recently and when he was asked his three wishes by the interviewer, he responded, "to go home, to have a house made out of candy, and to see a rainbow every day." Pretty simple.

"Do you still sleep with the light on?" is a powerful question because it strikes at the heart of a victim's uncertainty, hypersensitivity, vulnerability, and capacity to trust other people. On top of that it suggests a degree of hypervigilance that is the product of mistreatment and abuse.

It is time that we turn the tide. It is time that we work toward having all these children feel comfortable being able to sleep in the dark knowing that they are protected, that they are cared for, that they are loved. Let them hear that they can turn out the lights – and that there are adults who care.

It's also time that some other people become hypervigilant. To the abusers - to those who argue that the children bring it on themselves because of seductive behavior - to those who foolishly claim that kids consented when statutory and case law clearly proscribe this as a defense - we say to all of them "things are about to change."

This is where we come in. This is where, as Wiesel suggested, we must overcome the indifference that could infect us. We must have an expanded role and publicly advocate for abused and neglected children in ways that transcend our commitment to the provision of quality services. We have to continue to position ourselves at Perkins as the leader in the discussion of prevention techniques and treatment modalities for the children we serve and others who have been abused. Beyond that, I think we have to get the message out about our absolute disgust at the horror of child sexual abuse.

I am not talking about little catch phrases like "zero tolerance." Tolerance shouldn't even enter the discussion. Revulsion, repulsion, disgust, and outrage must be the response and we must convey that to everyone with whom we come in contact. I think we must turn the tide and have those who would abuse children and those who defend their right to do it become hypervigilant and unsettled because they know we consider them the predators that they are.

It's not about hate – it's about justice. It's about elevating the tone of the conversation and having adults who abuse children and those who defend their actions held accountable for their actions not only in the criminal and civil sense but also in the eyes of society as a whole. There is no unfettered First Amendment right to advocate for the wholesale rape of children – and that's exactly what some are doing. Children can't consent to sexual activity and any adult who abuses them should do so with the knowledge that the full force of the law and the norms of society will confront them when they are discovered and that strict and swift punishment will follow.

It is time for a shift. The little boy I spoke about who has to sleep with a light on, and thousands, maybe millions, like him - both children and adults who have been abused - must finally be able to turn out the light, go to sleep, trust, be happy, hopeful, and live their lives the fullest. To those who have perpetrated these horrible crimes – to those who defend their right to do so - and to those who create environments and put abusers in positions to accomplish their horrible crimes, we say, "things have changed!"

If we are doing what we must to wipe out the epidemic of child sexual abuse, we will no longer have to ask the kids or adults who were abused, "do you sleep with the light on?" Rather we will warn those who victimized them to "sleep with the light on."

To those who abuse and rape children, we would counsel them, "sleep with the light on." To those who defend their right to do it, we say, "sleep with the light on." To those who by their actions enable them to hurt, brutalize, and victimize children, we say to them "sleep with the light on. Your day has come."

We will know we have made tangible inroads when the rapists, the defenders, and the enablers are unsettled, hypervigilant, and aware that society will not tolerate their behavior, the cavalier view of children as vehicles and tools of sexual gratification, or those in authority who don't have the moral courage to take action to ensure the safety of children. When they are nervous, unsettled, and fearful of what is to happen, then we will have finally turned the tide and conquered indifference.

Our advocacy for children will be successful not just when children can turn out the light and sleep in peace but also when the predators and their allies have to turn *on* the light because they are feeling the guilt, the sting, and the uncertainty of what the future holds for them.

Our admonition to all of them must be one that is forceful and clear – not threatening and intimidating – just forceful and clear. Our admonition must simply be to let them know that, what they have done, they have done at their own peril. Our admonition must tell them that their time has come and that abuse is not only not tolerated but outrightly regarded as a wholesale disgrace.

Our admonition must simply be: "sleep with the light on."

2003-2004

The Nun was Right:
Lessons from the Church Crisis for Leaders and Managers
Wachusett Chamber of Commerce
March 26, 2003
Janeway Education Center
Lancaster, MA

According to recent calculations done by *The New York Times*, the church sexual abuse scandal involves more than 1,200 priests and 4,000 minors over the past 50+ years. The fact that it went on, the fact that it went on as long as it did, and the fact that even after it was uncovered the response was still an in-your-face, "we'll call God's wrath down on you if you keep poking around in our business" approach can be instructive. It can teach a lot to those of us who are involved in the administration and management of human organizations – businesses, schools, agencies - that are made up of people engaged in some enterprise whether it's producing goods and making money or helping others.

The February 12, 2003 *New York Times* carried a story about a New York grand jury investigation and subsequent 181-page report that asserted that the Catholic Church's Diocese of Rockville Center (which takes in all of Long Island beyond the New York City limits), while attempting to portray itself as helping victims, was instead engaged in a concerted effort to protect abusive priests under investigation. The piece cites specific instances where the diocese's interests appear to be more protecting its own personnel than the interests of those taken advantage of. This is a direct quote from the *Times* article:

> "In one instance the official (a priest-civil lawyer who ostensibly heard victim's complaints) told a parish employee, who reported suspicious behavior, that the priest would be sent for treatment, the report said."

> "What about the boy?" the employee asked.

The grand jury report said the official replied: "it's not my responsibility to worry about the boy. My job is to protect the bishop and the church."

The article goes on, reciting another vignette from the grand jury report:

> "In another case the lawyer-priest told a nun, who had intervened, that a meeting with the victim was a waste of time because the statute of limitations had expired, the grand jury said."

According to the report, the nun responded with an epithet and said, "These people are hurting. Why do you care about the statute of limitations?"

If I understand it correctly and, if you'll permit me to read a little into the nun-priest verbal exchange, and because in my line of work I've become something of an expert on "epithets" and expletives, I'm going to make an educated guess about what was said.

I would extrapolate from the conversation and the context, that the nun's response to the insensitive comment about how a meeting would be a waste of time, was to employ the time-honored expletive signifying disbelief or possibly doubt about the speaker's sincerity. Consequently, I postulate that, when the priest said a meeting was not necessary because the statute had run, I think the nun's answer was: "b-------."

You see – it fits. It fits perfectly. Even without having the grand jury transcript as a primary source, I think I'm on pretty solid ground based on the linguistic context. I think it's a reasonable conclusion on my part.

I also understand that for many of you who know the good sisters this is a whole new world for you. I must confess that in my 16 years of Catholic schooling I never heard a nun talk like that. As a matter of fact most of the nuns I knew would, without any hesitation, smack you silly if they heard *you* use that language. The fact that I have just repeated the expletive should lead you to another conclusion as well. The long-term efficacy of corporal punishment is questionable at best because, as you can see, while they always smacked me for saying it (and other objectionable expletives as well), I'm still saying it!

But - you know what – objectionable or not - the nun's description was right. "Sister Tell-It-Like-It-Is" hit the nail on the head, the bull's eye, a home run - whatever. She's right. And she's my kind of nun. She's had it with the duplicity, the secrecy, the damage control, the lack of leadership, and the sheer examples of bad judgment amid horrific acts of abuse and she's saying what's on her mind.

She can't stand b------- and I say God bless her! The nun was right.

What went on is exactly what she said it was. But we can learn a lot from this whole sordid episode. Most of all we can learn what *not* to do when you are confronted with a problem. We can learn how *not* to manage an organizational crisis. We can learn by looking at the Church's mishandling of this. We have all been or will be faced with some public crisis at some time – a toxic spill, an OSHA fine, a quality issue, a union confrontation, a sexual harassment case, bad publicity surrounding the separation of a disaffected, dishonest, or unhappy employee, or a thousand other unpleasantries that leaders and managers are called on to deal with.

Donna Morrissey, the Boston Archdiocese's official spokesperson, admitted last week that the scandal was a "public relations nightmare." Information was not shared with her and she had "constraints imposed on her." The *Boston Globe* reported that in a speech last week Morrissey noted that "mistakes were made in handling the crisis" and that "no one foresaw its dimensions."

A crisis can happen. It's whether you are proactive and reduce the chances of it happening and how you deal with if it does happen that make the difference in the long run. There are many examples of American businesses which, when faced with potentially destructive crises, addressed them as best they could and went on to reclaim their reputations. The Union Carbide disaster in Bhopal, India in 1984 quickly comes to mind. We now have in the church an example of an organization which made things considerably worse after the initial revelations of the problem.

Over 10 years ago I authored an article titled "Preventing and Dealing with the Nightmare: Sexual Abuse in the Residential Setting." As with so much I write, it received widespread acclaim from the six or eight people who actually read it, four of whom were relatives, and two of those whom I suspect were either lying or had reading levels insufficient to understand any of it.

In any event, in that piece I attempted to exhort human services CEOs and managers to do a number of things to prevent sexual abuse from ever happening and, in the event it did, I made suggestions about how they should respond. The recommendations transcend a sexual abuse crisis, however, and really form the basis of a solid crisis prevention and management plan generally.

If you'll permit me, I'll quote. I said:

"The best solution to dealing with sexual abuse is to create an atmosphere which eliminates the possibility of it ever happening or, at least, reduces the odds. Administrators must create the proper tone, develop procedures with prevention in mind, be alert to (client) reports and cues, and practice open, accessible management."

In essence what I was recommending was that right from the beginning employees understand that there is no room for misbehavior or abuse of any kind. I recommended that screening, interviewing, and the overall process of employee selection take special account of potential abusers. I counseled readers to be aware of the "cult of silence" where people cover for each other and lie for each other. I then recommended that all reports be taken seriously and investigated promptly and that management avoid an "ivory tower" style of leadership. I then suggested that they use what management experts Peters and Waterman had counseled years earlier - MBWA – "management by wandering around."

The archdiocese's HR people or seminary admissions people were horrible in the screening and selection processes and worse in supervision. There was no employee expectation about what constituted good behavior and, quite the contrary, as abusers were protected, I'm certain the word got out that there was little to fear from ecclesiastical or civil authorities if one were caught. The cult of secrecy and silence, long a Church characteristic, was no more evident than in this crisis. I think it's probably fair to say that, if the Cardinal wasn't reading Peters and Waterman, he certainly wasn't reading me and wasn't tuned into what was going on in the field of management generally.

I have come to these conclusions not solely based on personal opinion and experience but through a reading of some of the recent post-scandal literature. James Carroll, Eugene Kennedy and George Weigel have all published books or updated previously published works since the scandal erupted in full form a year ago last January. While they tend to have a theological bent to their calls for reform, I view things through an organizational and management lens, although Kennedy does a superb job of talking about organizational structure.

Well beyond disgust at the actions of the abusers and skeptical that any of the current church leaders has the intestinal fortitude, talent, desire, or will to change things, I have recently gravitated to the institutional, cultural, and organizational factors that allowed this all to happen. Maybe by viewing this as an organizational failure in addition to a human and personal failure (which indeed it is) we, as people who work in and run organizations, can make sure our own organizational crises do not result in our own undoing.

Carroll talks of a culture in the church of "silence, denial and dishonesty" and says, "The loss of *credibility* is destroying the very structure of the church." Compare that to several business crises over the last few decades that were handled well. Remember the actions of Johnson & Johnson, the makers of Tylenol, when the first tampering and poisoning occurred? They dealt with it by recalling all the merchandise, acknowledging their vulnerability and maybe even passive culpability, and subsequently revolutionized the packaging of medication nationwide.

How about the makers of the "new" Coca-Cola over a decade ago? After they introduced the new product, they saw it wasn't as well received as the old, and then started re-producing the old one as "classic Coke" - along with the new one - in response to consumer concerns and complaints. Talk about eating crow! But it did wonders for their credibility and perceived responsiveness to customers.

Right now, McDonald's is searching for new ways to market itself to make its products healthier in order to recover lost market share of about three percent, its first quarterly loss in history recorded last January, and to renew itself and to return to the golden years of the golden arches. These three companies took vigorous, up front actions when confronted with crises that could have meant their destruction as organizations. This morning's *New York Times* carries the story of a major administrative shakeup going on at the U.S. Air Force Academy in Colorado following revelations of long standing mishandling of sexual abuse complaints.

Unlike those organizations the Church has resisted calls for acknowledgment of wrongdoing and reforms of its ways. It has largely ignored the groups that have sought to help it change and generally relied on outmoded, anti-democratic procedures for climbing above the fray in the hope that it will all pass and all will be well again. Full-scale denial. Events of the last year suggest that this is simply not going to work and some degree of responsiveness to customers, to use the mercenary term, should start to happen if the whole organization is going to avoid implosion.

From all observations the church has no intention of "repackaging" itself like Johnson & Johnson, acknowledging error like Coca-Cola, or searching for new ways to bring back those it lost as McDonald's has. To those who sniff at such a suggestion and say, "it's a church - not fast food," I would simply remind them that good management is built on good human relations and that it is as much a part of church management as business administration.

Carroll points out that patriarchy is the dominant mode of organization and intolerance of internal dissent is characteristic of the church. Most management experts would counsel us that such a leadership style and stiff resistance to change are not conducive to healthy organizations that will survive in the future. You judge for yourself. Top down management that never listens to internal criticism is doomed when it comes to avoiding crises and dealing with them when they occur.

I think it's fair to say that Cardinal Law's style of leadership and that of many of his fellow bishops was paternalistic and not open to any intrusion by others. His decision-making style appears to be traditional as I suspect is true of most of these prelates. He had very little desire to use current management techniques in the running of his organization, if indeed he even knew such techniques existed.

The culture of the Church in many ways is a culture at odds with America – not just the medieval, patriarchal, anti-democratic stance it takes but the whole idea of discouraging inquiry and dissent as well. Kids in this country - maybe to a fault - are taught using inquiry methods in school and are encouraged to view things *differently* as a way of arriving at knowledge and truth. The church discourages that.

American culture, for better or worse, is distinctly different from the Roman Church's way of doing things that worked well in the Middle Ages and even well into the modern period but which seems to be eroding as it confronts crises now. I think a lot of what we have seen in this scandal exploding the way it has is an indication of how difficult it is for a medieval, patriarchal culture to survive in a society that values openness, participation, democratic leadership, and the ability to criticize and, when necessary, to dissent.

Cardinal Law's counterparts have learned little from the crisis. The culture they are steeped in, so long a part of the Church as an institution, will not easily change. Even now, some continue to use the "get the wagons in a circle" approach. In New York, Cardinal Egan's spokesman recently noted that a request for a meeting with him by an alleged victim of a priest abuser was not likely to happen. A *New York Times* article last month noted that the Cardinal has "a policy of not meeting with victims."

So - he hasn't learned much - and this from a guy who's already in hot water for mishandling earlier abuse cases in Bridgeport. That kind of intransigence in the face of documented evidence that such a style simply will not work also suggests that this is far from over.

The mentoring or succession process used in the Church also enhances the likelihood that others will act like Cardinal Law. They will because they trained under him and worked for him. The bishops of Manchester, New Hampshire (where the attorney general unleashed a scathing report in early March); Green Bay, Wisconsin; Brooklyn, New York; and the aforementioned, grand jury-criticized diocese of Rockville Center on New York's Long Island are *all* headed by Law mentees or protégés. The expanse of his power and influence was incredible and extended well beyond Boston. Consequently, so did his management style and techniques. Those he trained can only be expected to act as he did. They know no other way. Mentoring is great when the mentor is great, but the opposite is true as well.

Eugene Kennedy notes that within a short time of finding out that Cardinal Bernardin of Chicago had pancreatic cancer, Law was positioning a virtual unknown bishop to move to an archbishop position and then to Chicago as his choice to succeed Bernardin. That kind of succession plan is great when the guy (or gal – but in this case always guy) is a talented, forthright, skilled leader, and manager. It doesn't work so well when he's less than forthright and riveted on protecting the organization at all costs. He passes that on to those he's trained and they can be expected to behave similarly when they hold positions of authority.

So - what have we learned? I think we've seen that any organization that is committed to damage control in the first instance is making a mistake. Damage control is clearly a worthy organizational objective, but it shouldn't precede or replace acknowledgment of a problem and swift attempts to rectify the situation and assist those whom the organization has injured.

We have seen that leadership style has a great deal to do with the outcome of crises. Forthright, honest dealings are still the way to go – painful though they may be. We have also seen that one of the favored techniques of managers, mentoring, has its shortcomings when the mentor has shortcomings as well.

Finally, I think we've learned that when a crisis strikes, it's not always clear who's on your side and who's not, and who the good guys and bad guys are. Not everyone who criticizes you is out to get you and not everyone who tells you to "tough it out" it is your ally.

There's an old story that I think supports what I just said. It's the story of a vulnerable little bird - a sparrow - out on the frigid tundra in

Russia years ago, cold and freezing. The Russian army was passing by and stopped for a break. One of the soldiers noticed the freezing bird and in a gesture of compassion and kindness, bent down, scooped up some of the warm manure his horse had just deposited, and packed it on the bird. The squadron soon left.

The bird was ecstatic, figured he would survive, and began to whistle and chirp. His chirping was noted by the next troop that stopped for its break. One of the soldiers thought the bird's chirping signaled discomfort at being packed in all that dung. The soldier also in an act of kindness, knelt down, cleaned all the manure off the bird, and then departed.

The sparrow soon froze to death.

The moral of the story is threefold:
(1) The people who get you into it aren't necessarily your enemies,
(2) Those who get you out of it aren't necessarily your friends, and –
(3) when you find yourself up to your neck in s--- - don't just stand there whistling!

The *Boston Globe* wasn't Cardinal Law's enemy and those who told him to hold fast weren't his friends. And while I don't think he stood there whistling, he didn't understand the magnitude of the organizational crisis with which he was faced as suggested last week by his own spokesperson.

His leadership style and the culture of his organization all worked against any resolution of a problem that had been festering but kept quiet for years. His mentoring of others now in authority suggests that the scandal will continue to spread. It could have been different, but he and his organization couldn't change and see what was happening all around them. They continued with outmoded, insensitive strategies that made it all worse. They always appeared to be protecting the organization instead of the people injured. It was the wrong way to do it.

The nun was right.

Perkins
1987-2003: A Report

Teamwork!

I became a foster parent last year to three young brothers who were scheduled to be discharged from Perkins into separate foster placements. They were among the most compelling cases I had seen in the more than decade and a half I have been here. These three guys are bright, charming, engaging, "street smart," and truly hold great promise for the future. Their positive personal characteristics are counterbalanced by a history of alleged physical and sexual abuse and a lifetime of neglect, which resulted in numerous allegations and substantiation of horrific conditions and incidents of mistreatment.

Despite all that they retained uncommon resilience and a zest for life. Clearly "wise guys" some of the time, they are also sharp, insightful, and pretty funny. They have individual and collective senses of humor that I find delightful since I have always maintained that humor and an ability to see light beyond the darkness, are key ingredients for eventual success.

The three brothers (ages 11, 10 and 8 years) and I recently visited with their mother near Boston and, as we traveled through their hometown, they regaled me at each corner with stories of brushes with the law dating back to when the youngest was no older than four or five years of age. A week later two of the boys were having dinner at a restaurant with me and my daughter, an assistant district attorney here in the Commonwealth, and the subject of their past exploits came up again.

They recounted one episode that occurred while they were still living at home and spent a fair amount of time on the street. It concluded with their being taken off the roof of a Dunkin Donuts store after they had climbed up there. Somewhat amazed that a four-, five-, and seven- year-old could find themselves in that predicament and would then have to be removed by the police, my daughter inquired.

"How did you ever manage to get up on the roof in the first place?" she asked.

The youngest's response: "Teamwork!"

And so it is here at Perkins as well. *Teamwork* is responsible for the astounding record of accomplishment in this organization over the last 16 years. The building, the growth, the expansion, the diversification to serve new populations – are all parts of an amazing record of achievement made possible by a collaboration and alliance of Board, staff, community, benefactors and the kids and adults we serve. We believe in what we do and we do it as a team.

A National Reputation

When the JCAHO surveyor was here last summer for our reaccreditation, he noted in passing how pleased he was to be able to finally visit Perkins and see firsthand how we had achieved our *"national* reputation." It's no secret that I'm the greatest cheerleader for this place, but even I was momentarily taken by surprise by his assessment that Perkins is now viewed on the national stage as a great success and model for others. I was content to view us as the statewide or even regional leader in the work we do, as we clearly are, but I was delighted to hear that others see our influence as well beyond that.

The danger of doing a recap on the occasion of my 16th year anniversary at Perkins lies in the possibility that there might be some subliminal suggestion that the significant advances and tremendous accomplishments during that time are somehow the exclusive product of my management. Nothing could be further from the truth.

All that has happened here has happened because of the combined hard work and collaboration of a Board willing to take reasonable risks, a staff totally dedicated to what we do, a community that supports our good work, benefactors who provide the resources to help us, and kids, and adults who have achieved behavioral, academic, and social goals and, thus, stand as living testimony to the value of what we do.

A review of the last 16 years is worthwhile if we better understand how we achieved the status characterized by the JCAHO surveyor. However I undertake such a review with the caveat that it represents more that a stroll down memory lane and with the strong admonition that I am only *one* player in this amazing story of phenomenal growth, expansion, improvement in the quality of care, and overall success. We believe in what we do and we do it as a team.

A Recap

By 1988, Perkins had recovered from a period of malaise and declining enrollment and had achieved approval or re-approval from the states of New York, Maine, New Hampshire, New Jersey, Vermont, and Pennsylvania in addition to the existing licensing and approval from Massachusetts and Rhode Island. In years to come we would also receive students from Connecticut, Washington, D.C. and Florida into the 766 program.

The therapeutic horsemanship program, one of the first innovations we introduced into the program was already up and running for a year by 1989. Its success over these last 15 years, culminating in the current construction of an outdoor riding arena behind the barn in 2003, has been one of the components that sets us apart from our competitors.

In 1990, Perkins opened its first off-campus community program in the neighboring town of Clinton. **The Clinton Community Program** on Chestnut Street operated in rented space that we would later purchase and subsequently re-sell and which became the basis for the Adult Services relocation to Clinton at the Barlow Center in 2001.

In 1990 as well, the **South Campus** building at 380 High Street Extension in Lancaster was purchased and for several years was used for classroom space for older kids. In 2002 it became purely administrative space when the classrooms were moved back to the main campus to the new Janeway Education Center.

In May 1990 in what would be the first of eight buildings built, purchased, or acquired by donation, a three-bedroom home, **Friends Hall**, was constructed on the campus for Perkins adults who were approaching their senior years and required an increased level of care. Friends was our first attempt at a life care, staffed apartment program that would blossom years later into Davis Manor. Made possible by a generous gift of the family of Charles P. Gilbert, it is a tangible reminder that Perkins remains committed to our residents of many years even though a change in the core client population has taken place.

In December 1990, as a result of the generosity of Edward Barlow, former owner of Werber & Rose Furniture in Clinton, the **Barlow Center**, a 40,000 sq. ft. building on four floors, was donated to Perkins. In the intervening 12 years we have constructed: a full service dental clinic; a center for Clinton's senior citizens; the office of the local state representative; four community-based apartments for developmentally disabled adults; a state-of-the-art training center for staff and community use; and an industrial laundry to serve all our programs.

In 1992, Perkins was honored by the Clinton Area (now Wachusett) Chamber of Commerce as **Business of the Year** as it became one of the largest employers in the area. By 2002, Perkins was the second largest employer in the Wachusett Chamber region with over 360 employees.

In 1993 the **Centennial Fund** was inaugurated marking the school's upcoming 100th anniversary three years later. The campaign resulted in substantial upgrades to the campus. In 1993, Perkins was accredited for the first time by the Association of Independent Schools in New England (**AISNE**), a major step forward and a validation of the progress that had been made at the school.

In the same year the **Hymes Swimming Pool** adjacent to the Grover Hermann Center was completed. The three-lane, 50 ft. long pool was housed in a building that also included locker rooms, shower rooms, lavatories, pool office, and lobby area.

The pool was followed the next year, 1994, by the construction of the **Pappas Home**, a 12-bed residence for young boys, which came as a result of a generous bequest from the late Anna Pappas. Subsequent renovations and an addition were completed through the interest and generosity of Anna Pappas's sister, Christina Miggas. The school later became the beneficiary of the bulk of Mrs. Miggas's estate when she passed away in 2001. She left specific instructions that the proceeds were to be used for the Pappas program.

During the last decade the existing residences, Weymouth, the Manor, White Hall, Curtis Hall, the Duplex and Friends Hall have all undergone major renovations. In 1995 Perkins opened two community-based, staffed apartments in the Oxford Court complex in Clinton.

In 1997, Perkins opened **Friendship Place**, our first expansion into a population that was determined by age rather than specific special need. Although most of the clients at this adult day health center in South Lancaster had Alzheimer's Disease or other dementia, many required intensive day services because of infirmities due to age.

Friendship Place did well for five years but was closed in 2003 due to inadequate funding and a falling daily census. We still conduct a day program for our elderly residents at Davis Manor, but the community portion of the program was phased out in August 2003. Also in 1997, Perkins achieved a major milestone with its accreditation by the Joint Commission on the Accreditation of Healthcare Organizations (JCAHO).

In 1998, the **Hymes Fitness Center** was built completing an athletic complex composed of the Prentiss Gymnasium, the pool and fitness center. The center has been a popular addition to the campus for students and staff as well and the Clinton Senior Citizens and other community groups also have regularly assigned times during the week.

In 2000, building on our earlier experience with Friends Hall, our home for elderly developmentally disabled residents, and Friendship Place, our day health program for the elderly, Perkins opened **Davis Manor**. The facility came largely as a result of generous gifts of Louise Halsted and Jean Brigham, sisters of Denise Davis, a resident at Perkins for 75 years.

It was important that elderly residents who came to Perkins when they were children (one as young as six months old) be able to live out their entire lives in the familiar surroundings they had come to love. Denise enjoyed her brief time at this state-of-the-art assisted living facility. She passed away quietly in October 2000, only a few weeks after the home's opening.

In 2001, the aforementioned renovation of the Barlow Center was completed. It resulted in the creation of four apartments: two two-bedroom and two three-bedroom apartments serving ten adult residents. Some of them attend a day hab program at Farmer's Cottage on the main campus while others are involved in a contracted enclave work arrangement with Dunn & Co. and Legacy Publishing Group, two successful Clinton businesses.

The crowning jewel of the Lancaster Campus, the **Janeway Education Center**, was opened in 2002. The facility contains 15 classrooms, a modern library, beautifully appointed dining room and acoustically excellent auditorium. In addition to meeting the needs of our academically able student population, the Janeway facility, named for a family of multi-generational supporters and leaders at Perkins, is now a popular community site. Dinners, conferences, elected representatives' town meetings and concerts have all been hosted at Janeway. Other supporters of the facility included the Fieldstone Foundation, GenRad Foundation, and the George H. and Jane A. Mifflin Fund. Two wings of the building are named, one for benefactor Christina J. Miggas and the other, the education wing, for June Raymond, a long time staff member.

The Memorial Building, Wyman Center, and Hermann Center have all undergone substantial renovation and modernization so that the standard set by the new Janeway Center became the standard of excellence for the all the remaining education buildings. All classrooms are now air-conditioned and equipped with the latest technological and audio-visual advances.

Development: A Board Priority

The Friends of Perkins annual fund was inaugurated in 1988 and virtually from the beginning this Trustee-focused appeal has become the cornerstone of our fund-raising efforts, which also include appeals and proposals to Foundations and corporations. The annual fund has continued every year, even in the years when the capital campaign, the Centennial Fund, was up and running. In 1991, Perkins hired its first full-time Director of Development, T. Nathanael Shepherd, testimony to the Board's commitment to fund-raising and a realization that the task had grown to substantial size.

Since 1987 the School's endowment has risen from $2.3 million to almost $7 million. The endowment has experienced the ups and downs of the stock market but has benefited greatly from the estates of John Bowman (1992) and Christina Miggas (2002).

Since 1987 we have lost several trustees who were key supporters and decision makers in the School's formative years. We mourn the loss of former Board Presidents Elinor W. Janeway and Edward L. Anthony II and Trustees Rachael Bayles, Paul Caplan, Herbert Hayden, Paul Hunkins, and William R. Dolan, Jr.

Indicators of Growth

Facts, figures, and data tell the story of the phenomenal growth and expansion at Perkins. In 1987 the staff totaled 140; today it has risen to above 360. Perkins is the second largest employer in the nine towns covered by the Wachusett Chamber of Commerce. Below is a comparison summary of 1987 and 2003.

FY 1987 vs. 2003

	FY 1987	FY 2003	Change $$	%
In millions (except enrollment):				
Fund Balance	$2.4	$11.1	$8.7	363%
Total Assets	$3.4	$20.9	$17.5	515%
Fixed Assets (net of depreciation)	$1.8	$11.7	$9.9	550%
Endowment Fund (at market value)	$2.7	$6.7	$4.0	148%
Operating Revenue	$2.4	$16.9	$14.5	604%
Payroll and Fringe Benefits	$1.8	$12.5	$10.7	594%
Average Enrollment:				
766 Residential	34.0	94.5	60.5	178%
Adult Program	20.0	17.0	(3.0)	-15%
766 Day Program	0.0	41.0	41.0	
TIAA-CREF Matching contributions	$15K	$176K	161.0	1073%

Strategic Plans

    Since 1994, the Board has engaged in successive strategic planning initiatives as well as directing ongoing monitoring of progress in the interim. The 1994 plan titled *Blueprint for the 21st Century* and the 2001 plan titled *Perkins: Planning for the Future* have served as guides for continued innovation, entrepreneurship and continued growth and development. The Board's commitment to ongoing planning has been the hallmark of our continuing success. New programs and services including a licensed mental health clinic, extended school day and day camp programs, and mergers and collaborations are part of this thinking. It remains an exciting process.

Accreditations

We remain one of the few human service providers in the country to be accredited by both a regional independent schools accrediting body (AISNE) and the Joint Commission on the Accreditation of Healthcare Organizations (JCAHO). During the last year we have been re-accredited by both of these bodies.

Conclusion

What had been a successful, though struggling, residential school for children and adults with mental retardation has today become a multi-service organization serving diverse populations of people with special needs. The 766 residential and day programs specialize in services to children with mental illness, many of whom have been mistreated, neglected, or abused. Our adult program, though smaller than 16 years ago, is specially geared to the needs of adults with significant cognitive limitations. Similarly, our elderly program focuses on the needs of senior citizens with developmental disabilities, Alzheimer's and dementia.

What we do today at Perkins is bigger and better and we are doing it all for populations that in 1987 we never thought we would be serving. That expansion is a product of organized, systemic planning as well as a sincere desire to expand to meet the emerging needs of new groups who require our services and the enhancement of services to populations we had already served.

We believe in what we do, we know what we want to do in the future, and we make it all happen. Individually, we are committed to the mission and, collectively, we excel at making our mission a reality. The national reputation we have achieved has come about because of our belief in what we do - and teamwork.

Two of the brothers I spoke about at the outset were having breakfast one day and, while I was out of the kitchen area, I was still within hearing range. The conversation (one of the ones I can repeat in polite company!) shows us how forcefully you can state your case when you believe in something.

Jay: (To his brother who is reluctantly eating his scrambled eggs.) "Charlie says, if you don't eat, your brain isn't gonna work."

Brother: "Yeah. Right! What does he know!"

Jay: "If you don't eat right, you won't even know what one and one is."

Brother: "Jay, one and one is *two*!"

Jay: "See! - that's because you're eating."

Jay believed in what he was saying - even if he didn't get it all right. At Perkins we not only believe in what we do, but we get it right - and we do it as a team.

Teamwork!

"The Sea We Carry Within Us"
Perkins School Recognition Day
June 14, 2003
Janeway Center Auditorium

Over the years at Recognition Day, I have shared bits of wisdom with Perkins students and graduates from sources such as Robert Kennedy, Ralph Waldo Emerson, and G.K. Chesterton. I've also been known to quote the great American philosopher, Yogi Berra, and - one time - I surprised the President of the Board of Trustees with that year's choice of notables to quote. When I returned to my place on the stage, the President, an accomplished attorney, turned to me and said in amazement, "Miss Piggy?"

Each of those quoted, Miss Piggy included, was able to provide us with some insight or some window into their own thinking that I felt might be helpful to all of us as we celebrate Recognition Day, a day of renewal, accomplishment, achievement, maybe even survival, often against formidable odds. I salute our graduates today - those who are high school age and those who are considerably younger - because in your young lives you have begun to triumph over what has been thrown your way. Today I bring thoughts from three sources: Sponge Bob, some sixth graders in Boston, and a talented Hispanic poet - about life, courage, risks and danger, and surmounting problems and difficulties in our lives.

I have become a big Sponge Bob fan in the last year. I often find that Sponge Bob, Patrick, and Squidward have a way of cutting through the nonsense and getting to the heart of the matter. They often provide us with lessons worth learning. In one episode, as they are cavorting at the bottom of the sea, a huge fishing line and hook is dropped from above. It has a large chunk of cheese on it as bait. Counseled by Sponge Bob to avoid biting into what looks like a tasty snack, Patrick disputes his friend's warning and protests, "Hey, how could it be dangerous? *It's free cheese*!"

Well, my friends, I'm here to tell you that Sponge Bob was right. But there's a larger lesson here as well. In life generally what looks like free cheese can also have a hook embedded into it too. Not only, as we've heard over and over again is there no free lunch, but often what appears to be easy, free, and tempting is in reality nothing more than a hook, nothing more than danger. Free cheese and a lot of other things we encounter in life can be dangerous unless we make the right decisions and are wary of becoming attracted to things simply because they *look* good. Taking healthy risks is good and we learn from those experiences, but putting ourselves in the path of danger because something simply looks good is a recipe for disaster. To say "no" to what merely looks good takes courage.

The *Boston Globe* recently printed some comments by some sixth graders in the Boston Public Schools about what courage meant to them. One said, "Courage is something everyone has. Courage is a kind of strength that helps you stick up for yourself." Another student said, "To me courage means being able to face the sixth grade even though I'm supposed to be in the seventh grade, and not being scared people will make fun of me." Another kid said, "I think courage means to face the challenges in one's life. It can also mean to stand up for oneself or for others to do the right thing. Courage is a brave feeling that comes from the heart. Finally, a fourth kid said, "Courage means to me helping someone out with problems that they have. Courage also means having confidence in yourself and knowing that you can change someone's life."

All great definitions. Courage also is an ability to surmount and overcome the difficulties, personal problems, and bad experiences we have had earlier in life. I recently read a poem by Francisco Alarcon that I think talks of how no one else really knows what each of us goes through, how no one else knows what the poet calls "the sea we carry within us."

It's titled *Del otro lado de la noche, From the Other Side of Night.*

> Que decir ante silencio
> Las paginas que se quedan sin escribir
> Los libros en donde todavia
> Ni somos ni estamos ni existimos
> Esta vida condenada al olvido
> Aqui nadie sabe ni sabra
> Del mar que llevamos adentro
>
> What to say about silence
> The pages left unwritten
> The books in which we are yet
> To be appear exist
> This life condemned to oblivion
> Here nobody knows nor will know
> Of the sea we carry within us

Nadie sabe del mar que llevamos adentro. Nobody knows of the sea we carry within us. How true that is. No one else really knows what we think and how we feel. I'd like to think you've met a lot of people at Perkins who have tried to help you understand what you think and how you feel, but the sea represents something else too.

The sea we carry within us is also our potential – not who we are now - but who we are to be. The sea we carry within us will only become evident as time goes on and the waves of our personality, behavior, and accomplishments begin to hit the shores and touch others. Whether they will be roaring, thrashing waves or gentle ripples that barely caress the beach is not important. What's important is that we have to be willing to *make* the waves. We have to be willing to share the "sea we carry within us." We have to do that for ourselves, to achieve all that we can in life, but we have to do it in ways that will benefit others as well. We are confident today at Perkins that our graduates will do that. Some day you will truly know and others will benefit from the sea you carry within you.

So, there it is: advice from Sponge Bob, some kids in Boston, and some poet you never heard of. Beware of life's free cheese but have the courage to make the waves you need to make your life a success by helping other people. And - make those waves with the sea you carry within you.

The Fallacy of Inevitability
Perkins Staff Awards Dinner
August 21, 2003
Janeway Center

It's been said that Queen Victoria, the long-reigning English monarch, had very little tolerance for long speeches and sermons. A preacher who was scheduled to speak before her had been duly warned and made sure his sermon was short. Upon the conclusion of his remarks he resumed his seat next to the Queen who turned to him and said, "Sir, you were brief."

The minister quickly answered, "Your majesty, I never like to be tedious."

To which the Queen responded, "You were also tedious."

I will attempt to be briefer than usual and I hope not tedious but you can judge whether or not I succeed.

It's rare that I find in popular culture – movies, CDs, or videos – even the most current books – anything that I would remotely define as being inspirational or closely paralleled to the work that we do. Recently however I came upon a movie and then the book on which the film was based, which I think, are very closely related to what we do here and which have lessons that are very closely intertwined with our work here.

It's a story about overcoming the odds and how that's possible when one has the support of people who love you. It's a story about second chances and how everyone deserves them. It's a story about learning to understand who you are and how even after an early history of abuse and mistreatment you can surmount incredible obstacles and go on to be successful. It's a story about commitment and a firm belief that "you don't throw away a life just because it's banged up." It's a story of resilience and of hope. Finally, it's a story of how those who lend support to others who need it are often themselves elevated and transformed because of their efforts and have their good work validated by those they serve.

Charles Howard, Tom Smith, and Johnny "Red" Pollard defied the odds when they took what many thought to be a small, washed up, not particularly attractive, second-rate race horse and turned him into a champion, a winner, and an inspiration to Americans in the throes of the Great Depression of the 1930's. The horse succeeds against incredible odds. He fights back and throws off the labels put on him early in life. He learns to believe in himself and to triumph over his early history of mistreatment.

Howard was the owner of Seabiscuit; Smith was his trainer; and Pollard his jockey. At one point in the film Smith notes that Seabiscuit, after all the abuse in his early life "just needs to learn how to be a horse again." How often have we said that here? Kids wise beyond their years because of history and experiences they never should have had. Kids whose memories of abuse and mistreatment color their everyday lives. Kids who from an early age have struggled with mental illness, hallucinations, compulsions and fears. Kids who often must learn just how to be kids again.

Smith believed in Seabiscuit because of his fundamental belief that "you don't throw away a life just because it's banged up." Sound familiar. How many banged up lives do we see all the time? Howard, Seabiscuit's owner during his heyday and the man who would note that "everyone deserves a second chance," was head butted by Seabiscuit the first time he met him. Recall similar first impressions?

Another jockey described the horse as "mean, restive and ragged." Many had given up on him. In her book from which the film is derived, author Laura Hillenbrand noted that the average horse only lies down for five minutes at a time and normally does so at night. Seabiscuit, she wrote, "could keel over and snooze for hours on end."

"While every other horse at the track raised hell demanding breakfast, he slept long and late, stretching out over the floor of his stall in such deep sedation that the grooms had to use every means in their power just to get him to stand up." Hillenbrand goes on to say that, while Seabiscuit could be "amiable," his "career prospects were dim" and "he was as slow as growing grass." Many had simply concluded, "what's the use?"

How did they take this nag from the depths of despair to the pinnacle of success? The recipe as I see it was one of optimism, hope, commitment, and perseverance. The owner, the trainer, and the jockey all had high tolerance for misbehavior, a sullen attitude, and intransigence because they truly believed they could change it all. Each of them had also had some difficult experiences and been "banged up" in his lifetime.

However they were never sullied by what I have come to call the "fallacy of inevitability," the belief that past history, experience, mistreatment and abuse inevitably lead to unhealthy attitudes, unchangeable behavior, and a prognosis for a compromised life because we can never change things. The fallacy of inevitability could pervade our work but at Perkins we do an incredible job of resisting it.

Our Perkins staff teams, collaborative at all levels, are much the same as the triumvirate of owner, trainer, and jockey, which made a huge success of Seabiscuit. Our constant assessment of status and progress toward goals is not unlike what Howard, Smith and Pollard developed for the horse they were to make a champion. Not everyone who leaves here will be a champion in the same sense because they will not achieve the lasting fame of a Seabiscuit. But many of them will go on to achieve success in their own right because you have believed that was possible and did all in your power to make it happen.

My daily walks around here continue to reinforce for me every day that the fallacy of inevitability cannot take root here because we are unalterably opposed to thinking that suggests that the status quo for mentally ill and abused kids and developmentally disabled adults must remain the status quo. In the last few weeks I have watched incidents, momentary crises, and verbal exchanges. All involved dealing with poor behavior, but always with an understanding that what's going on in the moment is a product of a lot of things, the least of which may be behavior in the moment. Such behavior is learned - but it's not inevitable or unchangeable.

The staff's efforts this year, evident in the teen center, the student support center, the jobs program, the expansion of the after school and performing arts programs and a number of other innovations underscore our commitment to searching for new ways to best serve the damaged kids of Perkins. Those new ventures suggest to me that the fallacy of inevitability will never establish a beachhead here and for that I am grateful to you.

Nothing is inevitable when it comes to what we do. Kids can learn to trust again. Kids can be reassured after traumatic experiences. Kids can learn to encounter, grapple with and address serious mental illness that may be with them for a lifetime. That's not to say it's easy or that we are always successful. Neither statement would be true but the commitment to help kids to succeed is the basis for the goals we try to help them attain.

Toward the end of the school year, I had the pleasure of meeting with Brooke Fitzgerald's eighth graders and, as I noted at Recognition Day in June, I was pleasantly surprised at their insights into current events, literature and history. What precipitated that meeting was a book of poetry they produced about which I was intrigued and gratified. Their expressions of gratitude, love, and hope are further evidence to me that no one here accepts the fallacy of inevitability.

Listen as they say it because they say it much better than I. Their themes of gratitude to a mother, the imponderable elements of life, and how separation from loved ones is always dreaded (maybe because they have experienced more than the rest of us) all contain tremendous insights.

Brandon writes to his Mom:
I want to thank you for everything you did for me.
I want to thank you for bringing me to this world.
I want to thank you for taking care of me when I was sick.
I want to thank you for not getting mad when I yelled and screamed at you.
I want to thank you for putting me all together when I fell down or when I was hurt.
I want to thank you for cheering me up when I was sad.
I want to thank you for putting me where I am now because if you didn't we would never thank each other again.

Another student, Will, writes:
Once while on the shore

An old man said to me
"I can show you things of the past
And show you things to be"
I slowly stepped aside
I felt my hands were tied
By this old man I found
I was forever bound
To do a simple task
Of me the old man asked
"I feel my time is near"
Listen now and you will hear
Of things I will instill in you"
Things that are true
Things that are lies
Things withheld within your eyes
Things that burn
Things that freeze
Things that are said just to appease
A singing angel
A tortured soul
A creature underground, a mole
These are things he said to me
Forever the truth
Forever shall be.

Finally, Nick writes in a poem he has titled, "Beautiful":
I remember when you came around.
You would be sitting on the nasty ground.
She is such a beautiful one.
We always have so much fun
We hang out together all the time.
She is beautiful, and she is mine.
She is so beautiful and very smart.
I hope we never get pulled apart.

  That's what's going on here. They're telling us and they tell us all the time. Sometimes it's in their writing, in their poetry. More often it's in their speech and in their behavior. Sometimes it's in their anger. Sometimes it's in their tears.
  Regardless of how they tell us, they are always telling us how they feel, what they think, what they like, who they love. We get to read what they write, listen to what they say, to deal with their anger and dry their tears - and - sometimes it's not easy. We are sustained by our belief that they can and will succeed against formidable odds. We are sustained by our

belief that history and experiences do not inevitably create a compromised future.

The fallacy of inevitability does not pervade Perkins because we find both solace and inspiration in what we do. The lessons of Seabiscuit in some ways parallel our approach, but they also pale in comparison to the thoughts expressed by our own kids which often contain the themes of hope, change, and a longing for a better life. For it is those thoughts that truly say to us that what we are doing is good, is important, is worthwhile. It is significant that those thoughts come from them because they validate our work.

We are not paying lip service to some obscure philosophy. Our commitment, our perseverance, our hope, and our beliefs translate into meaningful change and healthy attitudes and behavior on the part of these very damaged kids. That should make us all feel real good. Things do get better for them. Nothing is inevitable when it comes to this line of work. The past does not exclusively determine the future.

At the conclusion of the movie, *Seabiscuit*, the voice over notes that the easy explanation to the story of Seabiscuit's success is that an owner, a trainer, and a jockey fixed a broken down horse. However, the narrator carefully suggests that there was also an ancillary benefit. The owner, the trainer, and the jockey didn't fix Seabiscuit at all. He fixed them.

I'm not prepared to say that any of us needed fixing, but I think it's fair to say that what goes on here day after day, as difficult as it can be sometimes, is good for all of us. As we see progress, improvement, and brighter futures, it encourages us to go on, to move forward, and to give our kids, adults, and elderly residents the best we possibly can. In the process we show them by our actions that the future is bright and that the inevitability of dark days to come is truly a fallacy.

Not Even Geoghan Deserved "Punishment" He Met in Prison
(Reprinted from *Worcester Telegram & Gazette*, September 19, 2003)

Weep not for John Geoghan but for what his violent death truly signifies. Sentenced to jail for preying on the young he himself became prey to a system that cries out for reform. In my own work I daily observe the effects on children of pedophiles who snatch their innocence and condemn them to a struggle, often lifelong, to undo what has been done. What they do is horrible, outrageous, and despicable.

So, how can I possibly muster any sympathy, any compassion for the likes of Geoghan?

There are larger issues than merely Mr. Geoghan's death. How does one argue that young children and others, including the severely disabled who require close supervision and care by others, are the only ones entitled to such treatment? How can you make the case that someone who is justifiably in state custody because of the commission of a crime is not also entitled to the same level of protection and vigilance as children and disabled adults?

It simply can't be done without challenging the limits of credibility. It's not about sympathy. It's about simple justice, decency and the dignity of other human beings. Hubert Humphrey's comment of years ago that the test of government is how it treats those in the dawn, dusk, and shadows of life (the young, the old and the handicapped) might easily be amended to include how government treats those in its custody regardless of how heinous their crimes.

It is not acceptable on any level for anyone to excuse what happened to this frail, very disturbed, old man by expounding some twisted logic about prison "culture." My management training left me with the distinct impression that organizational leaders have an obligation and responsibility to mold the "culture" of the organization and, where needed, to change it. Tacit acceptance of murder even of the most vile among us or cavalierly excusing such an act as an example of a time-honored hierarchy that puts child molesters at the bottom of the heap suggests that someone knows such a culture exists but does nothing to change it.

A prison guard who defecates in another human being's food does it because he is very disturbed himself. My guess is that he also does it because he gets to tell people about it and brag about meting out his own uniquely effective form of prison justice. But that also means others know. Such horrific actions are rarely solitary exercises since they are futile if they go unwatched or unmentioned. It becomes an irrevocable part of the lore of prison and enhances the status of those who are not to be trifled with be they inmates or guards.

Guards who act the way some guards allegedly did in this case are no better than those they supervise and may even be worse. Guards who enable, encourage or permit the more vicious among the inmate population to torment and torture others physically, emotionally or psychologically are themselves criminals. Supervisors and administrators who feign ignorance of such torment when it is common knowledge are themselves soiled by their complicity.

Maybe child molesters belong at the bottom of prison ladder, but they don't deserve to be murdered. And maybe – just maybe - there's one more rung on the bottom of the ladder, a rung beneath the surface, a subterranean rung so low it is unworthy of any kind of respect – a rung reserved for those who murder the defenseless or actively contribute to their deaths.

A Peculiar Breed Indeed
(Reprinted from *Lancaster Times*, December 11, 2003)

Maybe I was ten years old but I remember it pretty vividly - the casket draped in an American Flag atop the fire engine slowly wending its way down a Bronx street from funeral parlor to church. A New York City firefighter who died in the line of duty was always buried with full departmental honors.

Francis X. Casey, husband of Veronica (Conroy) Casey, was being transported in a procession of his fellow firefighters. Uncle Frank had eaten smoke in a bad fire and died of a massive heart attack. He was about 40 years old. I hadn't seen anything quite like it in 40 years. Not until last week.

It was sometime after Frank's funeral that I heard a comment for the first time, although I would later hear it again many times. "They're a peculiar breed these fireman," someone would say. "They rush into a burning building with no regard for their own safety in the hope of saving someone who they've never met. A peculiar breed."

Where do the Frank Caseys, and now the Marty McNamaras, come from? What a peculiar breed.

Peculiar indeed. Men who risk everything for other people. Sure, cops are "special" too – no question about it. Cops have a similar kind of camaraderie and close "brotherhood" to deal day in and day out with crime, violence and the darker side of life - But with fireman it seems *different*. It's not unusual for them to be multigenerational. Son follows father who had earlier followed his father to join one of the most selfless but dangerous professions imaginable.

They know the danger, but love the work. They only ask that others try to understand their love of their work - "the job" - and the danger at the same time. They simply love to do it.

What a peculiar breed - then and now. You can't help but notice the repetition of the same names over and over - McNamara, McLaughlin. It's brotherhood and true family. Some things don't change over time or because of a couple of hundred miles of geography. What happened in Lancaster and Clinton in 2003 is in many ways no different than what I grew up with in a city of 8 million people forty years ago. Men who risk their lives to rescue people they never knew and who lose their own lives in the process. Men who do "the job" selflessly. What a peculiar breed.

Marty McNamara of Clinton in 2003 is today's Frank Casey of the Bronx in the 1950's. They paid the ultimate price doing what they so loved to do. They only ask that the rest of us try to understand that commitment. What a peculiar breed.

Recited many times, most memorably by Senator Edward Kennedy in Worcester four years ago, the poem, "Gone But Not Forgotten," its author unknown, captures the sentiments of this peculiar breed who risk their lives - and their prayer for the rest of us:

> Brother when you weep for me
> Remember that it was meant to be
> Lay me down and when you leave
> Remember I'll be at your sleeve
>
> In every dark and choking hall
> I'll be there as you slowly crawl
> On every roof in driving snow
> I'll hold your coat and you will know
>
> In cellars hot with searing heat
> At windows where a gate you meet
> In closets where young children hide
> You know I'll be there at your side
>
> The house from which I now respond
> Is overstaffed with heroes gone
> Men who answered one last bell
> Did the job and did it well
>
> As firemen we understand
> That death's a card dealt in our hand
> A card we hope we never play
> But one we hold there anyway
>
> That card is something we ignore
> As we crawl across a weakened floor
> For we know that we're the only prayer
> For anyone that might be there
>
> So remember as you wipe your tears
> The joy I knew throughout the years
> As I did the job I loved to do
> I pray that thought will see you through

A "peculiar breed" indeed.

"Not Filling a Bucket But Lighting a Fire"
Perkins School Recognition Day
June 12, 2004
Manor Lawn

Two Questions

In past years at Recognition Day I've used my few minutes up here to further lighten the mood on this day of great celebration. So, I thought today for a change I would try a little something different and pose a question to our students. It's a question that has perplexed many people but one which, unlike a lot of life's questions - most kids have the answer to while many adults are in the dark. And here is that question. Actually it's two questions:

"Who lives in a pineapple under the sea?" (Sponge Bob Square Pants!)

"Absorbent, and yellow and porous is he?" (Sponge Bob Square Pants!)

Well – we're off to a good start. I recently noticed that our yellow hero is pretty popular in France as well. In addition to taking the obligatory pictures of the Eiffel Tower, Monet's gardens, and other landmarks, I couldn't resist snapping a photo in the metro (the Paris subway) of a billboard detailing the broadcast times of the man known there as Bob L'eponge.

The trip to Paris and the surrounding countryside was fascinating because I got to see some of it through the eyes of my ten-year-old foster son. It was truly an experience watching this guy, who hasn't spent a lot of time out of Massachusetts, as he encountered a different culture and language as well as the challenges of international travel.

Lessons from a Trip

As we began the 6½-hour flight, the Air France flight attendants gave us the usual safety tips and instructions about using the life jackets, oxygen masks, etc. in the event of an emergency landing in the Atlantic Ocean. Although meant only for me, he barked out in a tone that just about anyone nearby could hear, "Charlie, you really think this big thing's gonna float when it hits into the water? Yeah!"

I gently suggested that we discuss it later.

When we decided to go to the Orsay Museum in Paris to follow up on our trip to Claude Monet's home, he quickly reacted.

"Orsay museum! I wanna go. I wanna see some Clydesdales."

I didn't feel it necessary to review the fundamentals of Impressionist painting at that point since it was clear we had a good deal of other work to do.

On the return trip I packed a lot of my own stuff in his carry-on because he was able to get all his stuff in his big suitcase. He did have a few souvenir items in the carry-on, most notably some key chains he had bought for his brothers. My daughters and I proceeded through security, which as you know, is rather thorough since 9/11. The key chains in his carry-on set off every bell, whistle, and alarm in that section of Charles De Gaulle Airport. As the French guards pulled him aside, he pointed at me and screamed, "hey, wait a minute – all the stuff in that bag belongs to *him!*" I thanked him for his loyalty and told him how pleased I was that I wasn't truly in a jam with him.

What a real standup guy. He'd give me up in a heartbeat.

In addition to the lighter moments, he also learned a great deal. He experienced things he otherwise never would have. The Romans used to say, "experientia docet," experience teaches. How right they were! Seeing, feeling, and experiencing firsthand are as effective learning techniques as reading, theorizing, and imagining. More importantly, he developed a curiosity and desire to go further and to ask more questions about the country, the French people, their lives, and their history. That was obvious last week when we were discussing D-Day and the invasion of Normandy 60 years ago.

Education: Lighting a Fire

It was gratifying to see that the travel and experiences stirred in him a desire to find out *more*. It reinforced for me something that the Irish poet William Butler Yeats said years ago, "Education is not filling a bucket but lighting a fire."

Yeats was right. Education is not just filling your head and loading up to pass MCAS, the SAT, or even the bar exam. It's much, much more. Education is the cultivation of enthusiasm for learning over an entire lifetime. It's not just the act of *acquiring* knowledge, as important as that may be. It's the *desire* to learn as well.

He had his fire lit rather than his bucket filled. He learned a lot of things – that you should whisper certain questions on an airplane; that the Orsay museum has no horsies; and that you should assume responsibility for your own actions and not turn in your wonderful foster father for something he didn't do! However, he also developed an enthusiasm and desire to learn more and to go further to inquire about things that perplex him. For that reason alone the trip was an immense success. His fire was lit. If all of us are able to do that – if we are able to cultivate a love of learning, of eagerly confronting things about which we know little - half the battle is accomplished.

Keeping It Lit

In some of your lives you have had setbacks but you have resiliently responded and come from behind. Last week everyone was rooting for Smarty Jones to win the Belmont Stakes and become the first Triple Crown winner in 28 years. But, alas, it was not to be. A 34-1 shot, Birdstone, showed what it means to be a "come from behind" guy.

Smarty Jones had it all - and pretty much he's had it all along. He was two-thirds of the way to immortality – but - in the final moment - he couldn't pull it off. The horse who beat him was a "come from behind" guy who many had written off. He was a horse who pursued this race with eagerness, enthusiasm, and energy. He wouldn't step back when faced with a challenge. Birdstone had his fire lit but, equally important, he wouldn't let it be put out.

In your lives you will run into a Smarty Jones, or maybe a "Smarty Pants." Your ability to respond to that challenge will determine your degree of success. Some will attempt to put out the fire within you. Fight to keep it burning.

You must *want* to learn. You have to have the energy and enthusiasm to meet the challenge. We see examples all over this campus today and every day of young people who not only want to learn but who have also responded to life's challenges - the ones that have been thrown at them in the past and the ones they will confront in the future.

Education isn't filling a bucket but lighting a fire. It's also about keeping your fire lit when someone tries to put it out.

You're doing that and we congratulate you and we celebrate your achievements.

Keeping Babies Out of the River
American Cancer Society
New England School Health Summer Institute
Rocky Hill, CT
July 21, 2004

Introduction

Oscar Wilde the Irish writer and dramatist said, "some cause happiness wherever they go; others <u>when</u>ever they go." I hope by the time I'm done today you haven't put me in the latter category and are happy when I leave. Some of the information I will share today is less-than-positive, although, when we discuss today's kids, I think there's good news as well, That's true in large measure because *kids* are doing the right things but maybe *adults* aren't. Adults need to act to make things better for kids - and prevention and education should be our watchwords.

Prevention

Prevention is about education and both of them are rooted in hope. They're both about action but they're also about hope. Prevention stems from a sincere belief that we can make things better in the future by taking action now. Prevention and hope may even be synonymous.

Peter Gomes, the minister in the Memorial Church at Harvard University, says, "hope's greatest power is that it enables the present by embracing the future." We are enabled now by looking forward and believing we can change things. We have many positive examples of the success of prevention and public education. For instance we are light years ahead of where we were a decade ago in the prevention, detection, treatment and, ultimately, the eradication of cancer.

One personal note: my mother and her two brothers died of colon cancer; my father's sister did as well; two of his remaining brothers were treated for it and another one died of liver cancer which I always suspected started as colon cancer. With that kind of family history I am totally committed to early and regular screenings, which I have had each year or every other year from the time I was in my late 30's. I had pre-cancerous polyps removed several years ago and I can only guess where I'd be now if I didn't start those screenings when I did. I have also consumed a mountain of bran and a ton of flax seed in addition to pretty much eliminating fat-laden foods, a decision, I hasten to add, which came about when my gall bladder took leave of me about 10 years ago.

My parents took great solace in the fact that they provided for us. As children of the Depression themselves they took great pride in their ability to put food on the table, to have us take vacations at the seashore, and generally to give us a lot of what they never had. We ate eggs every day; on weekends we added bacon and sausage to that along with rolls and butter; and for most of the summer we went to a beach on Long Island where we stayed out in the sun for 8 to 10 hours a day, swam, and had a great time. I once facetiously thanked my parents for elevated cholesterol, sowing the seeds of colon cancer, and providing fertile ground for skin cancer – and mind you - they did it all in the name of good health. How times do change and what we know now!

Prevention works. Education works. Knowledge works. It's really that simple. Behavioral change can have huge dividends and behavioral change comes when we acknowledge the existence of a problem, educate people about it, and develop preventive techniques to address it. I know I'm preaching to the choir today, but I think you need to hear from time to time that what you're doing is valuable and worthwhile. It is!

Let me give you a quick thumbnail sketch of some of the things I uncovered, (although "found" is probably a better word) as I progressed with the writing of the book. My efforts hardly involved major investigative research. One of the things I quickly realized a few years back as I put the book together is the relative ease of accessing huge amounts of valuable information from the Internet and its rich variety of data-wealthy websites. I'd like to talk a bit about child abuse, poverty, homelessness, asthma, obesity, mental health issues and a recent study on the phenomenon of incarcerating rather than treating mentally ill kids. Along the way I will allude to some other issues such as teenage drug use and sexual behavior and briefly mention the recently noticed connection between television watching and attention deficits. Virtually all of these issues are fertile ground for public education and prevention.

Abuse and Neglect

Forty-seven out of every 1000 American children are reported to be victims of child abuse; 15 of every 1000 children are ultimately confirmed to be victims. 1996 figures which I recently updated from another source indicate that neglect is up to 60% of confirmed cases; physical abuse is up to 22%; sexual abuse represents 10%; and 7% of confirmed cases are emotional maltreatment.

The fatality statistics vary somewhat but pretty much everyone agrees that every day in this country, three children die of abuse and neglect. It is also noted that from 1976 through 1997 of all the children who were killed, "54 percent were killed by a parent, 30 percent by an acquaintance or other relative, and 15 percent were killed by strangers or unknown persons."

Poverty and Homelessness

When I finished the book in 2001, one in five kids in the U.S. lived in poverty; now it is one in six. One study compared poor and nonpoor children measured by a number of indicators such as health and cognitive outcomes. What jumps off the page is that child abuse is about seven times more prevalent for poor children; hunger is almost ten times as prevalent; and grade repetition is twice as common among poor children as are suspension and high school drop out rates. Poor children are two times as likely to have experienced a short hospital stay and three and a half times as likely to have lead poisoning.

What also needs to be repeated is that the rate of poverty differs dramatically among various racial and ethnic groups. The poverty rate for African-Americans is still about three times that for whites in the United States. Children are affected in larger numbers than adults because of multiple child families. According to the Census Bureau 32 million Americans, or 11 percent of the total population of 273.5 million people, lived below the poverty line in 1999. However, children are affected by poverty at a rate considerably higher than that because families include multiple children.

An issue closely related to poverty, homelessness, also has a profound impact on children. In addition to starting out life as low birth weight babies, homeless children have twice as many health problems, are more likely to go hungry, and have higher rates of developmental delay and, although findings have not been consistent, higher rates of depression, anxiety, and behavior problems have been reported in homeless children.

Asthma

Some health issues are also worth considering. There was a 160% increase in asthma in children under 4 from 1980-94, with kids up to 14 years of age experiencing a 75% increase. The current CDC/Center for Environmental Health website notes: "the prevalence of asthma in children (under age 18 years) is higher than it is in adults (age 18 and older). Asthma is the second most prevalent chronic condition among children. It results in approximately 14 million days of missed school each year. In 1980, 3.6% of children had asthma. By 1995, the prevalence had increased to 7.5%, or approximately 5 million children. The decline to 6.2% for children in 1996 may be the beginning of a new trend, or it may simply result from random variation due to survey sampling procedures."

A number of factors have been implicated including the tendency of kids to spend more time indoors now. They do it in homes that during the energy crisis were built to be either airtight or at least efficient users of energy. There is suspicion that dust mites proliferate in that kind of environment and that they bring about asthma attacks. It has also been noted that fragile, low birth weight babies, who in previous years did not survive birth, are living and growing into childhood. They are at risk for asthma and other respiratory problems.

The evidence seems to point to airborne allergens or irritants or other environmental factors. Cockroach droppings have been implicated as well as household pets and passive smoke in addition to the traditional villains: molds and pollen. Genetics can hardly be overlooked since parental asthma is a major determinant for offspring. Use of antibiotics for various ailments has been implicated in later development of asthma as has vaccinations for measles and whooping cough, which may bring about an asthmatic response later because they interfere with the immune response.

Foods seem to count for only a small part of the asthma attacks although there has been rising concern in schools about the large numbers of children who are now allergic, often in a life-threatening way, to peanuts. It has been suggested that more women seek out peanuts and peanut butter during pregnancy as a non-lactic protein source and that this somehow could be leading to hypersensitivity among children. At the moment asthma remains a huge health concern even though it has not hit epidemic proportions.

Obesity

"More children and adolescents are overweight in America than ever before, with about 12 percent of children and 10 percent of adolescents suffering from this condition," according to a 1998 report. Here's an update from a Child Welfare League of America report 1999-2000: 15% of children ages 6-11 and ages 12-19 were overweight; over 10% of preschool children ages 2-5 are overweight, up from 7% in 1994.

Kids, as many adults, eat too much and exercise too little. It probably will take several more years before the full impact of this hits home. Heart disease, high blood pressure, diabetes and stroke, all of which have been implicated as results of obesity, often show up in adulthood rather than childhood, although there has been an increase in childhood diabetes and hypertension as well. Sedentary life styles, less support for physical education as part of the school curriculum, fast food, and poor diet generally have all been pointed to, each with a good degree of justification, for the situation we now find ourselves in. There is a strong predictive relationship between being overweight as a child and being overweight as an adult.

Emotional and social problems instilled by a society that often worships "thin" in an unhealthy way, also cannot be underestimated but at the same time should not be overstated. While overweight people do not suffer depression and anxiety at rates noticeably different from their thinner counterparts, it is also interesting to note that, "depression and anxiety are caused by the weight problem and are usually resolved by weight loss."

The Executive Director of the Massachusetts Public Health Association noted in a piece in the Boston Globe that "societal and environmental pressures" have brought us to where we are. They include: the proliferation of unhealthy food and beverage advertising; increased television and computer usage; an abundance of fast-food outlets and a growing trend toward eating out of home; a reliance on automobiles; and a lack of safe and affordable physical activity opportunities.

At the moment there are no easy solutions to either the rise in the incidence of asthma or the virtual epidemic of childhood obesity. Both demand careful attention, study, and the development of preventive strategies to deal with them.

Mental Health

The Report of the Surgeon General's Conference on Children's Mental Health: A National Action Agenda, issued a few years ago, contained the statement that:

> The nation is facing a public crisis in mental health for infants, children and adolescents. Many children have mental health problems that interfere with normal development and functioning. In the United States, one in ten children and adolescents suffer (sic) from mental illness severe enough to cause some level of impairment.

My anecdotal information, confirmed by many colleagues in education, child welfare, and social services circles, suggests that there are more mentally ill children than ever before. Depression, anxiety disorders (including post traumatic stress disorder (PTSD) and obsessive-compulsive disorder (OCD)), attention-deficit hyperactivity disorder (ADHD), and eating disorders seem to be steadily rising, although I have not seen this definitively confirmed in any recent literature.

Unfortunately, there is still a lot of stigma attached to mental illness. However, there appears more and more to be a trend to recognize it in children. That is mitigated sometimes by assigning more "acceptable" diagnoses to children. Children who ten years ago would have been diagnosed "mentally retarded" are now designated "learning disabled," a more palatable label to some. More children are being diagnosed with Asperger Syndrome, rather than as autistic or mentally retarded, possibly because less stigma appears to be tied to a condition thought to be "high-level autism" or maybe because there truly are more kids with Asperger Syndrome and for that matter kids with mental illness generally.

Some of this comes purely from observation with special education populations of kids. However, it's confirmed by others in general education. A *Boston Globe* article contained a quote from a staff member at Yale-New Haven hospital who noted that in a five year period the hospital's emergency room witnessed a "nearly 60 percent jump in acute psychiatric cases among children and adolescents."

The Surgeon General's Report I just mentioned should be cause for alarm not only because it cites the problem at the startling rate of one in ten children suffering from mental illness, but because it goes on to say that only one in five who actually needs services gets it. It continues with a chilling statement about what we have to look forward to in the future:

> By the year 2020, childhood neuropsychiatric disorders will rise proportionately by over 50 percent, internationally, to become one of the five most common causes of morbidity, mortality and disability among children.

While the statistic cited is one from the World Health Organization and should open our eyes to the fact that this is a *worldwide* problem, we may already be seeing the increase here in the United States. In years past estimates of severe emotional disturbance in children were usually capped at around 5 per cent. Another study suggested it is more like 9 to 13 per cent. What's particularly scary is that it is higher than that with certain sub-populations of children, particularly those in the juvenile justice system. Some estimate that within that group the rate of mental health problems is "substantially higher than youth in the general population." The authors of that study later state that:

> With regard to diagnosable mental health disorders in general, research has found that most youth in the juvenile justice system qualify for at least one diagnosis. It is not uncommon for *80 percent* (my emphasis) or more of the juvenile justice population to be diagnosed with conduct disorder.

They go on to say that for the broader category of "mental health disorders" for youth involved in the juvenile justice system the prevalence rate is about 20 percent.

A related issue is one raised in a report, *Mental Health: Culture, Race and Ethnicity*, released by the Surgeon General in the summer of 2001. As with so many other issues, mental health needs are not the same among all racial and ethnic groups. The report states:

> racial and ethnic minorities collectively experience a disproportionately high disability burden from unmet mental health needs. Despite the progress in understanding the causes of mental illness and the tremendous advances in finding effective mental health treatments, far less is known about the mental health of African-Americans, American Indians and Alaska Natives, Asian-American and Pacific Islanders and Hispanic-Americans.

The Psychiatrist-in-Chief at Boston's Children's Hospital argued a few years back that we must look at the issue of childhood mental health in a much more comprehensive fashion than in the past. He emphasized a three part system that included (1) the need to "encompass the whole family, not just the individual child," (2) "universal access and coverage for both physical and mental health care," and (3) reorienting the care provided "toward prevention and early intervention."

A July 9, 2001, front-page piece in *The New York Times* documented the multiplicity of problems in the child mental health system. It noted that, "(w)hether caused by demographics or other societal shifts, a sharp rise in juvenile psychiatric emergencies has been reported in many states." The article also described in some detail the relatively recent phenomenon of the "stuck kid," the child who is unable to be discharged from a psychiatric hospital because of the dearth of step-down programs in residential and outpatient mental health services.

Incarcerated Youth with Mental Illness

A related issue is kids in detention facilities who are mentally ill rather than adjudicated juvenile delinquents or criminals convicted of adult crimes. I'd like to share with you now a study completed in Congress regarding mental illness and kids who are detained in correctional facilities. It was released earlier this month. It's entitled *Incarceration of Youth Who Are Waiting For Community Mental Health Services in the United States*.

The Findings of that 2004 report include the following rather startling conclusions:

- "Two-thirds of juvenile detention facilities hold youth who are waiting for community mental health treatment. (Get this: In 33 states, youth with mental illness are held in detention centers *without any charges against them.* (My emphasis) Youth incarcerated unnecessarily while waiting for treatment are as young as *seven years old*) (My emphasis)
- Over a six-month period, nearly 15,000 incarcerated youth waited for community mental health services.
- Two-thirds of juvenile detention facilities that hold youth waiting for community mental health services report that some of these youth have attempted suicide or attacked others.
- Juvenile detention facilities spend an estimated $100 million each year to house youth who are waiting for community mental health services.

What an outrage! Talk about mass violations of constitutional rights! Whatever happened to trial by jury prior to confinement in a correctional facility. Tens of thousands of kids in this country are incarcerated right now and they have committed no crime. Their only "crime" is that they are mentally ill. Our presumed sophisticated and educated society will not make provision for services and treatment and chooses to lock them in detention facilities. Absolutely medieval – but unfortunately it is reality.

We need to do much better in educating the public to the nature of mental illness that today is still vastly misunderstood. People today easily acknowledge that illnesses of the pancreas, liver, cardiovascular system - even the reproductive system - require medication to have those organs or bodily systems function correctly. However, they cringe when one discusses neurochemical imbalances and dysfunction of the brain and medications needed to sustain *that* bodily organ. Insulin, beta-blockers, even Viagra, have achieved acceptance, but Prozac, Zoloft, and Clozaril are suspect. How sad! It's truly mind-boggling and frustrating at the same time. We need public education about mental illness and we need it quickly.

Attention Deficit Hyperactivity Disorder (ADHD)

According to the National Institute of Mental Health, ADHD "is the most commonly diagnosed psychiatric disorder of childhood, estimated to affect 3 to 5 percent of school aged children. There are a number of different types of ADHD focusing on either the "inattention" aspect of the condition or the "hyperactive-impulsive" aspects of it, and then the two combined.

The causes of ADHD have been hotly debated over the years and there is pretty much agreement these days on a number of possibly factors including neurotransmitters, perinatal problems and heredity. ADHD does seem to run in families and boys are diagnosed at a rate four times that of girls. The treatment can be pharmacological, most often with Ritalin, the use of behavioral techniques, or some combination of the two.

A *Boston Globe* article a few years back describing a new $6 million government study of Ritalin opened with the following piece which is as much a statement about the prevalence of ADHD as it is the extent of the use of Ritalin: "nationwide, doctors write an amazing 11 million prescriptions annually for the brain-stimulant Ritalin." For parents, teachers, and others who work with children, ADHD reached huge proportions years ago and continues to be an issue faced every day.

You know better than I the extent of the problem easily seen in the numbers of kids to whom you administer medication on a daily basis. When my foster son was getting ready to go to Nature's Classroom, a weeklong nature exploration program in the public school he attends, I was somewhat reluctant to let anyone know he was on any medication. I attempted to judiciously and discreetly give the prescription vial for the week to the person running the program as the kids were lining up near the buses to begin the trip. She merely motioned to a huge cardboard box nearby and said, "Oh, that's fine, all the info's there. Just throw them in the box." As I did, I couldn't help but notice that the box was just about full. It looked like every fifth or sixth kid was on some kind of medication.

I'm not sure what all that means other than I do know that a lot of them need those meds and for many it's the difference of being in school or not. There is probably some degree of overprescription but we are maintaining kids in public school programs today who never would have been there in years past. For some their medication has been their salvation.

Media

In the book I dealt with media's effects on children and I hadn't planned to get into it too much today except to mention some findings a few months back regarding the relationship between television watching at a young age and ADHD. Derrick Jackson of the Boston Globe noted: "A new study in the journal, *Pediatrics*, found young children who watch television are more likely to suffer attention problems." He went on to note: "the study of 1,300 kids found that 1-year olds and 3-year olds who watched just one hour of television daily had 10 per cent more risk of attention problems by age 7 than children who watched no television at all."

So, there's an easy one for prevention enthusiasts – we need to reduce or eliminate the amount of time babies and toddlers are planted in front of the electronic babysitter. I would also direct you to the Kaiser Foundation report entitled *Zero to Six*, which explores media's effects on younger children.

Depression

My purely anecdotal information, observation, and experience suggest that there has been a measurable rise in depression in children and adolescents over the last decade. Epidemiologists have reported the rate in adolescents to be anywhere from 2.5 percent to a little over 8 percent.

In random groups of adolescents and young adults who are not considered to be "special populations," there is regular discussion among themselves of depression and which medication an individual is taking. While some might dismiss that as a "cultural," adolescent response to life's pressures, there is clearly more to it than that.

Experience suggests that there are more children and adolescents than ever before who experience unipolar (major depressive disorder) and dysthmic disorder (mild depression). In severe cases of depression there are clear links to suicide, which continues to remain one of the leading causes of death in adolescents and young adults. The National Institute of Mental Health website had some valuable statistics and information on suicide in children, adolescents, and young adults:

- Suicide was the 3rd leading cause of death in 15 to 24 year olds (12.2 of every 100,000 people).
- Suicide was the 4th leading cause in 10 to 14 year olds, with 298 deaths among 18,949,000 children in the age group.
- For adolescents aged 15 to 19, there were 1,817 deaths among 18,644,000 adolescents.
- The gender ratio in the 15 to 19 age group was 5:1 (males: females).

An interesting footnote for those who work with kids: the report notes that older people, who have the highest suicide rates of all age groups, have a tendency to go to their personal physician in the month prior to the suicide, which allows for the doctor to "eyeball" them and possibly treat them for depression. Kids have no such inclination and don't go to doctors at anywhere near the rates that the elderly do, so that the possibility of forestalling suicide attempts is severely reduced. That's important for school-based health professionals to know. Their observations about kids' mental states can be crucial from a preventive perspective.

The report also suggests limiting access to firearms particularly in those who appear prone to depression or substance problems. It also notes that school programs that focus on suicide may increase distress and are of questionable efficacy. The best prevention at the moment seems to lie with programs that have a wider mental health focus and which deal with substance abuse, coping skills, and behavior generally, rather than zeroing in on suicide itself. We should also not discount the probability that a lot of what are labeled car accidents may in fact be "suicide by car."

Eating Disorders

The anecdotal evidence of widespread prevalence of eating disorders in college dorms seems to be quite persuasive. While not exclusively conditions that affect female adolescents and young adults, the proportion of females to males with eating disorders is pretty much off the charts. It is not unusual to hear estimates that indicate the numbers of females to males is in the vicinity of eight to ten times as many. However, it is clear that the number of men with eating disorders is also increasing

The two major disorders, which have gained most notoriety, are anorexia nervosa and bulimia nervosa. In layperson's terms, anorexia is self-starvation and bulimia is characterized by bingeing and then purging the consumed food. Estimates of bulimia range up to 10 percent and anorexia up to 3 percent in young women.

Again, we see the need for nutritional education as a preventive and for better understanding and therapeutic services for those who require treatment. The issue of diet is complicated since we are dealing with obesity at one end of the spectrum and eating disorders at the other. It is a challenge to formulate educational and preventive program to reach all the kids we must.

Thoughts

However, what we are looking at in virtually all these cases is the emergence of conditions that must be addressed now. In every one of these five cases, there is clearly something going on that was not going on twenty years ago. To ignore that is foolish since twenty years from now (but probably long before that) we will pay a heavy price both in terms of human suffering and economic hardship. All is not well.

Look at the successes we have had with education regarding safety issues, for example, use of seat belts and bike helmets. Look how unsophisticated it is in many communities to light up a cigarette. It's no longer cool to smoke in some places, although, in others, kids still think it is.

Education can foster attitudinal and behavioral change. It took time but it worked. When I completed the book a few years ago, I was encouraged by what kids were doing, or more accurately not doing, when it came to sex and drugs, but that may be changing. A recent *New York Times* Magazine article discussed the phenomenon of "hooking up" and the prevalence of oral sex by teenagers in a somewhat cavalier fashion. It allows them, as did a former President, to answer the question, "have you had sex?" with a straight-faced, "no." Well, I have to tell you, where I come from, it's sex. It may not be intercourse, but it's sex – and it has major repercussions from both emotional and health perspectives. No one knows that better than you.

In a presentation I did seven years ago, I said:

"The preventive component is working to make sure that issues don't become problems by identifying <u>potential</u> problem areas and then giving people the information, skills and tools they need for self-help. Prevention makes a lot more sense than waiting for the problem to develop and then having to treat it, resolve it, cure it, or eradicate it. As crucial as those are, they're usually quite a bit more expensive.

"When problems develop we clearly have to do each of those things. But wouldn't it be ideal if all social, economic, health and medical issues could be resolved before they blossomed into problems. We know so much more in the area of health care today. What seemed a decade or so ago to be intractable medical problems - high blood pressure, stroke, certain cancers - can now be prevented through diet, exercise, and life style changes. The alternative is to sit and wait for a problem to develop when family history and individual medical history suggest that the problem is virtually inevitable. We know that in the areas of child abuse, child safety, and substance abuse awareness, education and skills development all help in prevention of the problems.

"Prevention, unlike treatment, is very difficult to defend and justify purely on the basis of data. "How many "whatevers" did you prevent?" is a considerably harder question to answer than "how many colon cancers did you excise?" or "how many stroke victims went through rehab?" How do you come up with hard and accurate data on how many things you prevented? It's not easy.

"And - therein lies the problem. We can extrapolate from extant data that a condition may occur in a normal population and then compare that to a population that has been exposed to preventive programs and see if there's a measurable difference. However, that's never going to be as neat and clean as what our colleagues in treatment can do. They can cure. They can treat. They can resolve.

"Even though we may have excellent medical and health facilities, wouldn't it be nice if we could relieve some of their burden by preventing some of the conditions they work so hard to treat? Preventive programs stop problems from developing and, while in the long run that's certainly more cost-effective - let's face it! - it's not as dramatic.

I went on: "that said, I think we have to renew our efforts toward prevention. What this organization is doing is most valuable. It helps people and it keeps the overall cost of treatment down because there's a reduction in the incidence of health and social problems.

"Prevention programs also allow people to take control of their lives in ways that treatment programs do not. In a prevention program you as an individual control your own destiny through diet, exercise, life style, whatever it happens to be. At the point where treatment takes over, an individual is not going to decide the dosage of the medication, the frequency of chemotherapy, etc. Professionals will make those decisions, as well they should. The individual's part in decision-making will shrink dramatically as they cross into the treatment phase.

The work *you* do is important, needed, and, frankly, very much misunderstood and undervalued.

I continued:

"I think we will probably not be able in the short term to change the public perception about the efficacy of prevention programs simply because the more dramatic breakthroughs come in the medical, surgical, and research arenas. We may just have to live with that. However, we can rejoice in our own knowledge that prevention programs severely reduce the number of problems that will ultimately develop and which will require medical, surgical, and other treatments to resolve or cure them.

"One of the great frustrations I experience in my own work is that almost all of what we do involves the provision of services and treatment for children who have been horribly mistreated, neglected, and physically and sexually abused. I have seen children who were sexually abused as early as the sixth month of life; kids who have had all their fingers broken or who have been maimed in other ways by people who are supposed to love them; children who have caretakers who suffer from severe mental illness which makes them unfit as parents but who really do love their babies; children of agoraphobics; children who have watched parental suicides.

"While I think we do a wonderful job, I can't help but wonder how much more effective it would be if we could deal with the conditions and root causes of child mistreatment and neglect so that our kids never require treatment in the first place. In some ways, I envy you because you are able to get in on the ground floor and deal with issues before they become problems. It's so much more effective to proactively prevent than to retroactively treat."

Conclusion

The inspiration for the title of my 2001 book came from a story by James Carroll, a writer for the *Boston Globe*, who described the work of Kip Tiernan, the founder of Rosie's Place, the first shelter for homeless women in the United States. He talked about Tiernan's concern for the *causation* of problems as well as her better known commitment to programs which treat those problems. Carroll asked several questions:

> "What would you do if you saw a baby floating helpless in a river? You'd rescue it. And if other babies came floating down? You'd get help, and you'd rescue those babies too. If more and more babies keep coming down the river, you would organize rescue squads and foster homes. But at what point would your gaze turn upstream, and when would rage choke you with the question, 'Who's throwing babies in the river?' And what would you do then?"

"Treatment is about pulling babies out of the river and we need strong treatment programs in every community. There's no question that we have to cure, treat, resolve, and eradicate health and social problems in America. We have to pull the babies and others out of the river. But it doesn't stop there.

"What we also need to do even more is to go upstream and see "who's throwing the babies in the river?" Then and only then can we change the conditions and prevent the problems so that babies are never thrown into the river in the first place. The goal must be to keep babies out of the river."

I concluded the book by noting that we needed a lot of things for kids, but especially *two* things in the final analysis. The first thing we need is adults who will advocate for kids but also parents who will say "no." The Catholic Church clearly bears huge responsibility for allowing priests to abuse children and then covering it up, but I also think a culture of the time forced children not to talk to their own parents or, if they did, to have parents discount what they said or silence them. Thankfully that has changed. Most kids today know that no one should touch them incorrectly. Equally important, most parents would take swift and decisive action after a child's complaint.

"Some problems are adult problems - not kid problems. Divorce, poverty, homelessness, and the incarceration of mentally ill children are adult, sometimes public policy, issues. They are not within the realm of kids to solve. Kids have done better on issues of sex, drugs, and violence, the last one vastly overblown by the media as regards incidence.

"We must work to eliminate the evils of child abuse and neglect and we must also act to improve conditions so kids can thrive and flourish regardless of personal circumstances. Prevention is one of the key techniques for improving the lives of children in the 21st century."

President Kennedy once quoted Dante who said "the hottest places in hell are reserved for those who in a period of moral crisis maintain their neutrality." We have to act and act soon.

The second thing I concluded in the book was that what we need for kids is something I alluded to before *hope* - not optimism – but - hope. I think we have to be optimistic that we can change things but also have hope that, as we fail from time to time, ultimately we will prevail and will give kids what they need to succeed. It's not really a choice - we have to do it if we are committed to improving the lives of kids.

I don't know that I've ever quoted Haile Selassie, the Ethiopian emperor, but he said something about indifference and inaction that makes a lot of sense to me. Prevention is about discarding indifference and taking some action. He said, "Throughout history, it has been the inaction of those who could have acted; the indifference of those who should have known better; the silence of the voice of justice when it mattered most; that has made it possible for evil to triumph."

I think the same can be said about the conditions today's kids find themselves in. They are often not of their own creation. Adults can fix them. Adults can fix them if they are committed and if they believe they can make a difference.

Maybe it's not as clear as good and evil but it seems to me it's close. Babies will be kept out of the river, but only if we act now.

New Challenges, New Directions
Perkins Staff Awards Dinner
Manor Lawn
August 24, 2004

Some Things are "Stupid"

Two weeks ago I bumped into Josh, an eight-year-old from our Pappas Home, and his one-to-one staff in the lobby of the Hermann Center. He gave me a big hello and I complimented him on his new haircut. Natascha, the staff member, was trying to coax him over to the Memorial Building for some reason or other and was doing a nice job of laying out how they would go, what would happen and what he would get if it all went well. Josh had a different idea. He was willing to go, but he wanted to go on *his* terms and play with a calculator, as I recall, before he began the trek to Memorial.

Natascha again laid it out again, step by step, but Josh abruptly cut her off.

"We do not have a deal. That would be a *stupid* deal!" he said.

I must confess that I occasionally see things in childcare and child welfare circles that provoke a similar reaction on my part. In my role as a foster parent (which you are probably getting tired of hearing about) I see things that also strike me as "stupid."

Listening to the Customer

This past summer my foster son was in day camp and every morning and every afternoon I dropped him off and picked him up. On the first morning I was in a queue of cars – about 20 as I recall - and I could see that their system needed work. There was a delay as we sat and waited for someone to come up to the car, give each parent a clipboard to sign the kid in, then pull up and wait for the car door to be opened and the child let out. I gave it another day and - it was just as bad.

In any event the kid who greeted us each day was this energetic, engaging teenager with a huge smile who always wished me a great morning and fine day – a real personality kid. So I made up my mind that, while I was going to transmit my frustration about their system, which was absolute idiocy, it wasn't going to be to this nice kid who after all wasn't in a position to change it. I wanted bigger fish.

On day three the assistant camp director was out there with the clipboard signing in the kids from each individual car as the line of 20 or so parents waited and some fumed. When my turn came, I rolled down the window and in terms reminiscent of eight-year-old Josh, I said, "This is stupid. It was stupid on Monday. It was stupid again Tuesday, and it's stupid today." And it's going to be stupid until you change it." That, as you can imagine, has a way of getting people's attention and, while she said she would pass on my message, I was still sitting in the line every morning and afternoon for the next seven weeks. They changed *nothing*.

Later on in the camp season they sent the camp director over to my car to see if she could convince me that their dumb system could work if we were all just patient. I have never mastered the art of patience, unfortunately. At 8:28 a.m. one morning, she asked me in the most condescending, pedantic tone, "do you know that we open at 8:30?"

I assured her that my watch was in working order and I reminded her that, if she looked at all the wasted time of the parents, and, if I used a calculation similar to hers for parents who picked up kids late from extended day, (i.e., $5 a minute) I would soon be sending her a sizeable bill for my time at the end of the summer.

What they never learned at that camp was that a parent's perspective could be valuable and that sometimes you need to re-evaluate what you're doing. Other parents I spoke to were similarly frustrated, but there was never any recognition that the camp staff heard any of the criticism and was going to change one inch from their position. They didn't care one iota what anyone thought and that, my friends, is what's really stupid.

"There are none so blind as those who will not see," as they say, and it was clear to me that the day camp leadership and staff cared little for their customers who after all are the parents as well as the kids they serve. They simply didn't get it and I suspect over time they will lose customers as a result.

Personal Perspective

I bring that example up because my personal perspective is informed by my own experiences, as are all of yours. I continually ask are we doing the best we can for kids here at Perkins. I usually come to the conclusion that we are doing remarkably well, largely because we remain open to the suggestions and ideas of others.

I am particularly concerned about how ready kids are when they leave here to re-integrate into family and community life in an orderly fashion. Are kids truly ready? I think our efforts this year on that score have been tremendously enhanced with the two new transition positions that are focused on services to kids and families after they leave here. We have made a leap forward because we felt we could do more and could make transitions to community life more likely to succeed.

As a foster parent I see how kids who leave programs like ours often have a difficult time occupying themselves and using leisure time productively. Because they are scheduled - and around here that means being involved in a huge variety of activities - they rarely have learned to occupy themselves.

When my foster son realized that my Saturdays are often spent with journeys to exciting places like Shaw's and the dry cleaners rather than going to the movies, swimming, roller skating etc., he was amazed. Hey! -

that's what people do on Saturdays. I still don't think I have really managed to convince him that he doesn't have to give me a full report of his whereabouts when he's in the house, the residue of his residential days where we need to know where kids are *all* the time. I've told him many, many times that I don't care that he's going to the bathroom. Just go. But he continues to tell me so I know where he is.

As an aside, he still has some interesting ideas that I can't blame on his residential experience. When he announced to one of my daughters that we had been out shopping for clothes and that he got a lot of stuff, he went on to say, "and I got underwear. I haven't worn underwear in five years."

From a spot not too far away, I said, "Whoa, back up a bit. Why do you say things like that? I do the laundry here and I wash several pairs of boxers every few days."

"Boxers aren't underwear," he says.

"Yes they are," I say.

"Are not."

"Are too."

"No," he concludes in his wonderful, airtight way of thinking, "underwear is little and it has no legs!"

I've given up on trying to formulate an ironclad, universally accepted definition of underwear and I am simply happy that he uses it even if he doesn't understand what it is.

His older brother had a similar illusion. When I foolishly found myself in a similar conversation with him two years ago, I mentioned that there were things called briefs as well as boxers.

"Yeah, well I want boxers. I don't like briefs. They *bend* everything."

Since I never want to be a party to anything getting bent that shouldn't, I simply decided to forego further debate. On this score I am clearly a beaten man. These comments and discussions go on all the time.

He was delighted that he made the lacrosse team in the spring and came home to tell me. "The good news," he said bursting with pride, "is that I got my uniform."

"The bad news," he went on, "is that I'm N*umber 2*!"

Our residential kids at Perkins need to be saturated in more of life's little things and we have to work to de-program them from Perkins even after they have done so well. Sometimes all the de-programming in the world won't work and it's just a bad match when they get into foster care.

I'm reminded of a case this year where one of our young ladies, an urban street kid who was pretty "with it," was placed in foster care with a lovely, refined, cultured woman who clearly had the child's best interests at heart but who was soon overwhelmed by her behavior. The kid couldn't settle into the rural household where there was no cable TV and where she found the woman was a vegetarian while she was a confirmed carnivore with a clear predilection for Mickey D's.

The foster mother was quite willing to cook meat occasionally, but even so, there was clearly a bit of a disconnect here. How it all happened is anybody's guess. Everyone was trying to do the right thing but it was not going to work out. The young lady's language in describing her frustration was also the vivid, colorful, creative, and descriptive variety we have all come to know and love at Perkins but which I suspect wasn't often uttered in this house. It simply was not meant to be. The girl wasn't ready and neither was this very willing, giving lady who so wanted this to work. Our work is really more art than science.

New Challenges

One of the new challenges we will be faced with and rise to as we always have is the new state initiative to revamp the way residential services are offered. There is discussion and soon to be a formal request for proposals which will attempt to "unbundle," as they term it, services to kids like ours and then offer them in an increasingly community-based model.

The services will emphasize a strengths-based, family-centered approach targeting the triad of issues we deal with all the time: mental illness, substance abuse, and domestic violence. The thinking is based on a premise that a reduction in residential beds will fund the other services being unbundled. This is being pursued despite the fact that the needs are greater than ever, the intensity and acuity of the kids' disturbance is more evident than ever before, and the demand for beds is greater than ever before. The demand is exacerbated by a reduction in beds years ago when the state closed places like Gaebler Children's Center at Met State Hospital. Everyone forgets that.

As recently as two weeks ago (Aug. 9), the *Hartford Courant* reported, "officials of Connecticut Children's Medical Center told the *Hartford Courant* that psychiatric admissions have nearly tripled since 1998." The chief of psychiatry at Yale-New Haven Hospital said, "psychiatric admissions of children under age 18 have increased by about 10% every year for more than a decade."

The article went on to say that, "there is also a shortage of beds at residential facilities." My sense is that the trend noted in Connecticut is happening in Massachusetts as well.

Makes you wonder how anyone faced with that kind of information would be talking about further decreasing residential bed availability, doesn't it?

I have attended more meetings on this topic than I care to recall and I think that some of our staff is far out ahead of me on the philosophy that undergirds this approach. I am not going to argue with the *intent* of this change, since I think it is well founded. How do you argue against a family-focused, strengths-based approach? I do, however, question, how this can be accomplished given what I see all the time. It's an uphill battle that is worth the effort but we better be careful that a lot of kids aren't left out in the cold.

If you want to see how well a similar shift worked in New York go and see the large numbers of people who sleep on subway grates, on subway trains, or are in shelters. The vast majority of the so-called "homeless" are mentally ill. They're not in hospital wards. They're integrated in the *community*, the social experimenters will tell you - and they're right. They *are* in the community – in community shelters, subways, or doorways.

Regardless of misgivings by some, this initiative will steamroller on. Make no mistake about it. We will see different services provided here in the future. I'm not certain our residential census will go down dramatically in future years because we have a reputation as being the best program and the best facility in the state – a well deserved one I might add.

However, there might indeed be a reduction in residential beds at Perkins and we might find ourselves in different services that we don't currently provide. We already have initiated a Behavioral Health Department, which provides consultation for public schools regarding kids with emotional and behavioral problems. We are enlarging our capacity to take more day students with Asperger Syndrome and our after school program has taken in day kids who need services in out of school hours.

At the Board of Trustees level and with some leaders in the community, there is discussion of a possible child development center/day care operation. We are also talking about a group home to widen our spectrum of residential services in line with what DSS is thinking. Who knows? We may be doing our own foster care service at Perkins before long. If this proposed state idea is going to work it's going to take increased availability of desirable foster care placements to replace residential beds, something that has always been a problem.

There also has to be careful attention to balancing child protection and family-centered/strengths-based reunification of families. No one can rationally argue against doing everything possible to keep families together by capitalizing on strengths inherent in the family that can't be replicated elsewhere. However experience also tells me that some families can never be reunified because of the child protection issues present. If domestic abuse and drug abuse are present in the home, child abuse and neglect will accompany them. It's really that simple.

New Directions

We clearly will be moving in new directions and into new areas of service very soon. That will be driven not just by kids' needs but also driven by directives from policy makers and buyers of service in the field who after all "call the shots." What we have going for us is a quality academic program that returns kids to home communities with educational gains; quality programs in reading and character building; therapeutic riding; an excellent residential component; a state-of-the-art facility; and amazingly talented staff. On and on it goes.

Those things will set us apart. Our generally innovative approach will also make us stand out. What has been created here is a national model for child welfare programs. Even if we have reservations about "unbundling" services, to try to stand in the way of the train is not productive. We have the desire, talent and resources that few others have and we've shown that time after time. We will address this challenge and be stronger as a result.

Seventeen years ago this was exclusively a residential school for developmentally disabled kids and adults. There were 34 kids, 17 adults, and no day students - that was it. This year we topped out at 102 residential kids and another 60 day students – amazing. We also serve ten adults and seven elderly people at Barlow and Davis Manor. The kids are no longer developmentally disabled; they're mentally ill, in some cases neglected or abused, but many are very, very bright.

Seventeen years ago, Friends Hall, South Campus, The Barlow Human Services Center, the Pappas Home, the Hymes Pool, Davis Manor, the Hymes Fitness Center, the Janeway Education Center and the brand new indoor riding arena – nine buildings! - were all just *dreams.* However they were dreams that became reality because we believed and worked toward our goal. In 1987, this agency employed 140 people and had an annual budget of a little over $2 million; today, its employs 360 people, is the second largest employer in the towns covered by the Wachusett Chamber of Commerce, and has a budget of over $17 million.

My hope is that the dreams will continue, that we not lose our resolve, and that we continue to press forward in enlarging and improving our services to kids and adults with special needs and their families. We will do that:
- if we continue to take risks;
- if we have high expectations and never give up on kids;
- if we hope and truly believe we can make a difference;
- and, finally, if we keep our eyes on the compelling individual cases and kids in our care rather than generalizing and globalizing problems that could easily overwhelm us with their tragic proportions.

Taking Risks

As far as the first, taking risks, an example. Most of you baseball fans have heard of baseball's legendary Ty Cobb - but how many of you ever heard of Max Carey? In one season Max Carey stole 51 bases in 53 attempts – he succeeded 96% of the time! Ty Cobb stole 96 bases in 134 attempts. That's a success rate of only 71%.

But who remembers Max Carey? Nobody. Why? Because Carey played it safe – he didn't take risks. Cobb stole 96 bases, 45 more than

Carey - because he was willing to go beyond the sure thing. I think people here, Board and staff, sometimes get weary of the pace, the new programs, the building - but I believe that if you don't grow, you die. Most of us don't want to be associated with an organization that merely exists, takes up space, and year after year does the same thing with little change and a belief that everything is all right because no one is "rocking the boat." That hasn't been the case here and it's the reason for our success. We always rock the boat!

Expectations

Secondly, we need to have high expectations and build on kids' strengths as well as those of their families. When two parents were confronted at a teacher conference by a rather blunt teacher who told them their daughter would fail French they were taken aback. The teacher coldly said, "she's just too dumb to ever learn French."

Her father responded, "well, maybe the problem isn't *her*. I don't know much about teaching methodology and I'm certainly not fluent in French myself, but I guess I have to ask, "how do the dumb kids in France learn French?"

We want the best. We expect the best. We want to always improve. We want to stand out. Yes, every year there's something new, there's something different. That excites a lot of us but it exasperates others. The race can only be won by those who run not those who stand on the sidelines watching.

Hope and Belief in Making a Difference

We have to *hope*, one of my interminable themes, and we have to believe we can make a difference. In 1966 Robert Kennedy, who was then my U.S. Senator in New York, addressed a group of South African youth and exhorted them to consider the fact that one person can often change much in this world. Kennedy alluded to Martin Luther, Alexander the Great, Joan of Arc and Thomas Jefferson and went on to tell the South African kids that they could change things.

"These people moved the world, said Kennedy, "and so can we all."

He went on: "Few will have the greatness to bend history itself, but each of us can work to change a small portion of events, and in the total of all those acts will be written the history of this generation. It is from numberless diverse acts of courage and belief that human history is shaped.

"Each time a person stands up for an ideal, or acts to improve the lot of others, or strikes out against injustice, he or she sends forth a tiny ripple of hope, and crossing each other from a line of different centers of energy and daring, those ripples build a current that can sweep down the mightiest walls of oppression and resistance."

We have to have hope and believe we can make a difference.

Concentrate on Individuals

Finally, we can't always focus on the magnitude of the problems we face. Childhood mental illness, abuse and neglect are huge problems and can be overwhelming. Sometimes it helps to concentrate on individuals as a way to keep things in perspective.

Sometimes we can get overwhelmed when we think about the complexity of the illness, the magnitude of the abuse and the extent of the problems our kids have. We tend to group them and see how horrific the overall problem is and that's perfectly understandable, but I have found over the years that sometimes it's more motivating to concentrate on one, very telling, compelling case and use that as a way of trying to motivate yourself and change things.

A few weeks ago in the same Hermann Center lobby where I encountered Josh I sat down to talk to Danny, an 11 year old, who was crying, who has a terrible time coming to school, and who a staff member has taken to picking up at his home and bringing him here. The staff has been magnificent working with his fears, his depression, and school phobia.

We were finally able to get him to settle down and to begin thinking about going into class where, once he's there, he usually does pretty well. He stopped sobbing, breathed a little easier, his chest stopped heaving, and he rested his head in his hands.

I said to him, "see, Dan, you're already feeling better and when you get in the classroom, you won't be crying."

He looked up at me and said, "Yeah, but I'll still be crying on the *inside*."

"I'll still be crying on the inside." That sort of says it all, doesn't it?

It's easy to group all the problems of all the kids and to see the incredible amount of horror and pain we deal with, but it may be more effective to concentrate on *one* compelling, persuasive case as a way to motivate ourselves to move ahead, to change, to improve, and to continue to hold this place out as the model and standard of care we have always tried to be.

We can look at the vast numbers of horrible cases we deal with, the extent of the problems, the devastating effects of mental illness, abuse, and neglect - or we can concentrate on one case – on *one* kid.

Concentrate on *one* little boy.

The one who's "crying on the inside."

2005-2006

Q: Should residential program staff become adoptive, foster, or visiting resources for children in their programs?

(Reprinted from *Residential Group Care Quarterly, Spring, 2005, Vol. 5, No. 4*)

POINT: Staff with experience working with troubled children/youth are valuable resources as potential adoptive, foster, or visiting families for children in their program.

A group of kids is playing soccer on a beautiful autumn afternoon at a large school and residential treatment facility in New England. The staff stands on the sidelines and eagerly cheers on the boys, residents from two or three of the facility's homes on its 100-plus acre campus. Included are the three Vasquez brothers, Jack, Joey, and Jim, ages 8, 9, and 11. The "JVs," as they are known, will soon be discharged. One by one, they are scheduled to move in with a new foster father. He also happens to be the school's director.

The game isn't that rough, but one of the players is knocked to the ground. A whisper goes through the crowd of staff spectators, "Uh, oh, is that a Vasquez!" The staff wondered what an injury to one of the soon-to-be foster sons of the CEO would mean. Revenge? Allegations of lack of supervision? Mass firings? The possibilities were numerous and ominous. After all, these three were the foster sons of the boss!

As it turned out, the boy knocked down wasn't hurt. To everyone's relief, he wasn't a Vasquez, so the perceived threats to the staff never materialized. The vignette points out, however, a potential problem when a child welfare agency staff member (CEO or not) takes on the role of foster or adoptive parent for a child in the same agency.

Are there built-in problems with such an arrangement? Should staff be discouraged when they express interest in providing a more permanent family arrangement for kids in their care? Does it make a difference if the prospective foster/adoptive parent works directly with the child in question? What potential conflicts might arise? How will other staff react? How will other kids in the same program (many of them without families) react to seeing a staff member single out one child for personal attention and commitment?

Maybe it's just too complicated to deal with. The need to address all of these questions might suggest this is not a good idea. Maybe residential facilities staff should simply be barred from becoming foster or adoptive parents for kids in their facilities.

That's the easy answer, but as H.L. Mencken said, "For every complex problem, there is a simple answer. And it's wrong."

There are clearly potential problems with residential staff becoming foster or adoptive parents. Favoritism and conflict among kids or staff is possible, but that's no reason not to go forward if a staff member expresses sincere interest and commitment. The program team has to examine the request and see if it's a good fit and then put in place the necessary safeguards for the child, the prospective parent, and the other kids in the program.

It's important to remember that as the foster or adoptive plan unfolds and takes shape, another agency, usually the state child protective department or a contracted agency, will be involved. It can provide an additional set of eyes to ensure the placement is realistic and potentially successful. So, there's another safeguard.

Why foreclose on the possibility of having a person who is trained and has chosen child welfare work as his or her vocation become a foster or adoptive parent? It is counterintuitive.

Adults who have chosen child-oriented careers are obvious choices to be foster or adoptive parents. Personality, temperament, history, and interactions with kids would certainly be factors to examine, but it strikes me that people working with kids should have a leg up on foster or adoptive parenting.

Those of us in this kind of work have experience and a record of interactions with kids, factors often missing in people who volunteer to become involved with kids for the first time. Residential staff, steeped in practical experience, also has realistic expectations. They understand the complexity of kids who leave residential facilities. Untutored foster or adoptive parents, on the other hand, can be blinded to realities by their altruism—laudable though it may be.

A mismatch of parent and child is considerably less likely when the foster or adoptive parent has previous knowledge of the child and has made a decision based on experience and a belief that he or she will hit it off with this specific child. Often foster or adoptive placements start cold and are based on a vague feeling, thought, or inclination to do something to help a child.

Child welfare facility staff goes through a long, deliberative process based on the needs of a specific child (whom they know), and they are generally informed by their experience with children. Their decision is not based on a general feeling of wanting to do something nice for a child, but a feeling of wanting to do something for this particular child. In other words, the decision is child-specific.

What appear to be obstacles at the beginning can be worked out if the program team is closely involved, focuses on the needs of the child, and views the expressed interest of the staff member in the same way they would any other prospective foster parent. Vigilance, team collaboration, and careful attention to the needs of all involved, including the other children who are watching closely, can make it all succeed.

We owe it to children to have as many viable options as possible when it comes to foster and adoptive care. Trained child welfare agency staff are perfect candidates. One might even ask, "Who better?"

Why Catholic Education?
St. Mary School Dinner
Janeway Education Center at Perkins
April 28, 2005

Introduction

Fr. Tomasz called me several weeks back and posed a question.

"Charlie," he said, "do you believe in free speech?"

I said, "Sure I do."

"Good," he answered, "Because you're about to give one."

Those of you who know the Pastor of Our Lady of Jasna Gora, who doubles as Headmaster of St. Mary School, also know that he's got this wonderful, disarming way of getting you to do things. He never twists your arm. It's very high-level, sophisticated, well thought out strategy that inevitably results in your saying "yes" to whatever he's asked. I can't imagine they're teaching those skills in the seminary these days, so I have concluded that these must be street-smart skills developed on the streets of Poland.

If you conclude by the time I'm finished that you don't like what I had to say, you can - first and foremost - blame me. However, at the outset I have to tell you that, because I am a product of their instruction, you can also blame - in no particular order: the Sisters of Charity of Mt. St. Vincent; the Xaverian Brothers; the Marist Brothers; the diocesan priests of the Archdiocese of New York; the Irish Christian Brothers at Iona College; the Brothers of the Christian Schools at Manhattan College and, last but by no means least (the faculty of my alma mater, Fordham University) - the Jesuits. But, of course you already knew that - because the Jesuits get blamed for *everything*.

Education is a Wonderful Thing

There's a story that I think is apropos this evening. In the early part of the 20th century Bridget, the stereotypical Irish housekeeper, was being admonished by the lady of the house who was pointing out to Bridget that her work was not up to the high standards to which she was accustomed.

"Bridget," she screamed at her, "the dust is so thick on this bureau that I can write my *name* it!"

To which Bridget responded, "Aye, ma'am, and isn't education a wonderful thing!"

Education *is* a wonderful thing but I'm not here to educate anybody tonight. I thought rather I would simply try to provoke some thinking about education, Catholic education, Catholic education in this region, and, specifically, Catholic education at St. Mary School in Clinton and what that means for the future.

I choose to do that by asking the question, "Why Catholic education?" In recent months I think something of a renaissance has begun taking place at St. Mary School - a renaissance spearheaded by the pastor and the new principal and supported by members of the School Board and a newly founded group of Trustees who acknowledge that there has been a struggle over the years but who wish to look at the future with optimism, vibrancy, and enthusiasm. Some people must think that this is a time and an opportunity for St. Mary School. Are they right?

Statistics and Trends

The Church has gone through many changes these last 40 years and it is a very different institution than the one in which I grew up. Catholic schools have changed as well. In recent years and even recent months the news has not been good. Last month, the National Catholic Education Association reported, (according to a piece in *The Boston Globe*, March 30, 2005), that the population of kids in Catholic schools dropped from 2.6 million in 2000 to 2.4 million in 2005. The article went on to point out that, "national enrollment decreased 2.6 percent from the 2003-4 school year to the 2004-5 school year as 173 schools closed or consolidated." My guess is that those figures include only schools that actually closed this year not those that have announced they would close but won't actually do so until next year, which I know in the Diocese of Brooklyn, NY and the Archdiocese of New York is a significant number.

Oh – at the tail end of the article it noted that, "37 new schools opened." Amid the closings, there are openings. Amid the disappointment there are pockets of hope. I think St. Mary School is one of those pockets of hope that not only can survive but also can thrive if the *right* people, with the *right* commitment, come together at the *right* time, and determine that it's going to happen. I'll get to that later on.

In a graduate course I taught years ago I emphasized that there are a number of characteristics of schools that are judged to be "effective." Research has shown over the years that there are a number of factors and they include: Strong leadership, high expectations, an orderly climate, an emphasis on basics, and regular monitoring of student progress. Additional factors might now be included, but those are the ones that stick with me. Parenthetically, I would add a factor that, strictly speaking, is not a characteristic of the school, but to my way of thinking is clearly a determining factor in successful schools – parental commitment and involvement in a child's education.

I think we can see all these factors in St. Mary School and I think that's the foundation from which we need to build a stronger, vibrant, quality-committed school that is acknowledged as such in the region. If that sounds like "pie in the sky" it's because it may be. I believe that there is a future for St. Mary School because the basics are there and because what's evolving is a level of commitment that I think can be harnessed. That commitment can generate the energy and resources to improve what's there and make it better known, respected, and a viable option for today's kids.

Where Do Catholic Schools Fit?

I reject the idea that strengthening Catholic schools is a threat to public schools. It so happens that we are blessed in this area with wonderful public schools to which parents would be proud to send their kids. I sent my own kids to them. Because public schools in the area are good *doesn't* mean that the Catholic school option should go away however. Some parents want something more or something different and that option must be preserved.

Over a decade ago I wrote a guest column for the *Catholic Free Press* titled "Catholic, Public and Private Schools Need Support." While it's always dangerous to go back and read something that you wrote 10 or 12 years earlier because you might have to eat your words, I did it anyway. In talking about Catholic Schools as an educational option and, after reviewing the rise of those schools in New York City, I said:

"As alternatives themselves, Catholic schools affirm the importance of personal selection in education. Long before anybody talked about "school choice" and, certainly long before government chose to formalize it, complicate it, and produce conflict surrounding it, Catholic schools stood as a constant reminder that choice could and would work. The existence of alternatives should not mean conflict."

I went on to say:

"Supporters of Catholic schools should also be supporters of public schools and private schools. A strong educational system in the three sectors works for all of us. Although their individual missions and how they carry them out may be quite distinct, all schools have a common objective of creating an informed, skilled, humane and educated populace that will strengthen the democracy in which we live."

I still believe that today. I also think that Catholic schools have the ability and the option to teach values and form character in ways that public schools are often restricted from for constitutional reasons, because it can be viewed as proselytizing, which I'm not so sure I would dispute. However I think we all must be concerned that somehow universally subscribed to values are transmitted to students.

Whether you're a Christian, a Buddhist, a Muslim, a Jew, or an atheist seems to me to be irrelevant on certain questions. It's wrong to steal from others. It's wrong to hurt or murder people. It's wrong to rape women or sexually abuse children. It's wrong to lie, to cheat, or embezzle. They're all codified in our criminal and civil statutes. However, the message somehow gets muted in public schools from time to time because of the fear of potential litigation because people confuse character and values with religion.

Catholic schools have no such restriction and it seems to me they should capitalize on that capability and make the case loudly and strongly that we *are* teaching values to kids. Yes, we're teaching values - along with a strong academic emphasis on reading, math, language arts, science, social studies and technology education – but make no mistake about it - we're teaching values.

Are Kids the Problem?

I hear a lot about what's wrong with kids today and invariably I throw it back at people and remind them that what's wrong with kids today is by and large problems created by adults. The same day that the Globe reported the piece on Catholic education which I alluded to earlier, it also contained an article on the condition of today's kids focusing on the Child Well-Being Index, a measure of the condition of America's children. It supports what I've been saying for years. Kids are doing things right.

It's the adults that are screwing things up. Kids don't create poverty, homelessness, divorce, and domestic abuse. If young kids are obese and asthmatic, whose fault is that? The Globe article reported that true kids' behavior, as measured by adolescent and teen birth rate, drinking and crime, is improving. Adults are the ones who need to take action. Adults are in charge. We have a responsibility to control or intervene to assure kids behave in a safe, healthy, and socially acceptable manner based on values that we subscribe to. It's our responsibility, not the kids.

Steve Bailey, a Globe business columnist, raised an interesting question that I'll now put to you. Why did Reebok choose the rapper, 50 Cent, to sell their sneakers when he routinely is pictured with a smoking gun and extols the fact that he was shot in Queens, NY by other thugs who had a disagreement with him? The adults at Reebok are putting him forth as a sneaker salesman but in the process they enable millions of kids to look up to him and, I fear, emulate him and his message about violence and his views about women. Are you going to blame the kids for that? They may end up being like him – but - it's only because adults suggested they do exactly that.

I was actually going to read some of the lyrics from some of 50 Cent's songs, but I simply couldn't find one that I could recite because of the profanity, explicit descriptions of sexual acts, and extolling of violence. Most of you who know me know that I have a pretty high tolerance for street language and I don't blush easily. However, I have to tell you that this stuff is malignant – bad, nasty, racist, woman-bashing, violence-encouraging stuff.

Go to www.50centonline.com and read the lyrics that kids hear and then ask yourself why the hell would Reebok ever ask this guy to be their sneaker salesman. Why don't more people say we don't want that for our kids and – then - why don't we stop buying Reeboks to show we mean it?

Adults Need to Act

In short I think adults need to be in charge. We need to transmit to kids what our beliefs about right and wrong are. We need to direct them. We need to correct them. We need to love them, but we also need to set them straight when they veer off course, as kids inevitably will. A lot of adults won't do that. Adults are the problem – not the kids - and adults are the answer. That helps us to start answering the question, "Why Catholic education?"

Adults are also the answer when it comes to sustaining Catholic education. Kids will follow our lead and other adults will follow our lead if we are clear about what we are trying to do. There is clearly a role for Catholic education in the year 2005 and beyond and I think there is a definite role for St. Mary School in Clinton. I think St. Mary School can not only survive but can flourish - but to do that a number of things must begin to happen.

How? Four Suggestions

I have 4 suggestions and here they are:
1. Carve out a niche, maintain a distinct identity, and make it known to others;
2. establish clear goals and articulate clear expectations;
3. believe we can make a difference; and, finally
4. have faith and hope and it will all come together

Distinct Identity

As far as the first - a distinct identity - before we can let others know who we are, we have to know ourselves. We have to ascertain what's important to us, what we believe in, what we want out of life, and what we want for our kids. Identity comes from more than mere appearance. People may recognize you from your face, your house, your car, whatever it happens to be. But the question of who you *are* is a product of how you act and what you believe or, more accurately, how you act *on* what you believe.

When I was in Ireland several years ago someone explained to me the origin of Aran Island sweaters - you know - the ones they call Irish knit. Each has a different knot, braid, stitch – whatever the right description is - but it's more than mere design. It's got a purpose.

The way it was explained to me is that the sweaters were worn by Irish fisherman who went out to sea and all too often never came back. The sweater has the distinct braiding or pattern because the sweater might become the only way of identifying a fisherman whose boat had sunk or who was thrown overboard by a swelled sea. If he stayed in the water for weeks or months, he may not have had a face or any other means from which he could be identified. However the sweater signified a certain family or clan and he could be traced by means of it. He might have no face, but people would know who he was. That's worth thinking about. Will people know who we are by what we do? What you *do* is your Aran sweater. What is St. Mary's Aran sweater?

Catholic schools, in addition to prizing academic excellence and performance, also teach values. We hope and expect that graduates of those schools will be thinking people of values, people of courage, people who do the right thing. I'm reminded of the famous conversation between the American authors, Henry David Thoreau and Ralph Waldo Emerson. When Emerson came to visit Thoreau in jail while he was engaged in one of his many instances of civil disobedience, Emerson asked, "Henry, what are you doing in jail?

To which Thoreau responded, "Ralph, what are you doing out of jail?"

Does St. Mary's prepare kids to make the right decisions both as kids and adults. What is this school's niche and identity? Do others know that?

Goals and Expectations

Secondly, I think it's important to establish realistic goals and clear expectations for what St. Mary School will accomplish now and in the future. I'm not talking about the instructional program at the school. I'm talking about goals and expectations for those who want to see the school flourish. I'm talking about many of us. We need to clarify our short- and long-term goals.

Jesuit priest, Fr. Charles Allen, who I met several times during the time when one of my daughters attended Fairfield University, told me of an experience he had while explaining his short- and long-term goals. He and I both attended Columbia University for graduate school at different times and he said he created something of an uproar when he submitted his entrance application.

When the form asked for his short- and long-term goals, he did fine on the first question. His short-term goal was to be a high school principal of a Jesuit high school. However, when he got to the section on the application which asked "What is your long-term goal?" he wrote, "To know, love and serve God and to be happy with him forever in heaven."

Now that's what I call a long term goal!

We need to clarify long-term goals for St. Mary School and lay out a plan to make it happen. A good deal of great work has been done on a strategic plan and we may need to revisit it and amend it to reflect these new goals and aspirations for the future. St. Mary School will move forward but it's entirely possible it may not look the same or be configured the same way.

Believe We Can Make a Difference

Third, we also have to believe we can make a difference. I gave a talk last summer to a group of health educators from all over New England at a conference in Connecticut. At the conclusion of my presentation, the woman who chaired the conference gave me a starfish pin. She said, "It's for people who try to make a difference."

It's a bit hokey, I suppose, but basically the story behind it contains a nice message. There's a little kid at the beach who's walking along the shore. He picks up a starfish that has been washed up and is broiling in the sun and he throws it back in the ocean.

An old man comes up to him and says, "What are you doing?"

To which the kid says, " I'm throwing him back in so he doesn't die."

"You really think that's gonna make a difference?" says the man.

The kid looks at him and says, "It made a difference to *him*."

You can make a difference.

Faith and Hope

Finally, I think we need to have faith, hope and confidence in our ability to succeed. In a recent e-mail to Fr. Tomasz, I concluded by writing, "Spes, semper spes," "hope, always hope." He responded, "fides, semper fides," "faith, always faith." I'm not going to fight over which one is more important – it seems to me we need *both* faith and hope as we press on.

Former New York Governor Mario Cuomo put forth an example of faith and hope and confidence in a story he told of "Fishhooks" McCarthy, a shady politician on the lower East Side of Manhattan. Fishhooks happened to be a devout, daily communicant, although he had a reputation for taking liberties with the public trust. He hoped and believed in the power of the Almighty but was willing to put all he had into the effort. Cuomo related that Fishhook's daily prayer at a local church was: "Lord, give me health and strength - and we'll steal the rest." I'm not recommending that as a personal strategy mind you. I'm only putting it forth as an expression of faith and hope supplemented by sincere confidence in one's own abilities.

I'm not talking about mere optimism by the way. I'm talking about hope – and they're different. Peter Gomes, the minister at the Memorial Church at Harvard University, makes a distinction between optimism and hope. "Optimism is the belief that things will get better. Hope is what sustains you when they don't." Hope is what we need - hope and faith that our efforts will succeed.

Now - Why?

St. Mary School can survive and make a difference because it has the right people, who will make the right commitment, at the right time, Make no mistake about it, this is an uphill battle at a time when other Catholic schools struggle - but it can be a successful one if done right. It will involve the 4 things I just alluded to:

- forging a distinct identity and making it known to others;
- establishing clear goals and articulating clear expectations;
- believing we can make a difference; and
- having hope and confidence in our ability to succeed.

Having given you my recipe for *how* we go about this, I will now circle back to the justification for *why* we should do it in the first place, which itself brings me back to the original question I posed: "Why Catholic education?"

Why? Because Catholic education is good for kids. Character formation and values education are not exclusive of academic excellence. A well-rounded individual is sound of mind, body and soul. What did the Romans say? "Mens sana in corpore sano," "a sound mind in a sound body." We add to mind and body - soul, conscience, character - give it any name you want. I heard character defined a while back as "what you do when nobody's looking." For me the answer is very clear and totally consistent with what I've written and spoken about over the years and what I believe. Catholic education is good for kids. That's why.

I'm going to avoid the temptation to use platitudes about how precious our kids are and how we need to invest as much as we can in their academic, physical and emotional development. Periodically something happens which drives home that point in a way that can be startling, maybe even painful.

Yesterday at Immaculate Conception Church here in Lancaster a funeral mass was offered for a young lady, 17 years old, a student at Nashoba, who was tragically killed in a skiing accident a few days earlier. She was a vibrant young woman, a talented athlete from a great family, and all of a sudden her parents, her sisters, and her brother no longer have her. If ever there was a vivid reminder not only of the fragility of life but also the need to love our kids and take care of them for all the time we have them, this is it. It is unfathomable to bring meaning to the loss this family has suffered and yet it can serve as a reminder of how important our kids are and how much they mean to us.

Catholic education underscores how much our kids mean to us because it represents a commitment and investment in their lives and their futures. Catholic education is about academic excellence, but it's also about values and character and being a decent human being. In Catholic education expectations for kids are high. That is totally consistent with my own thinking about kids.

How Kids Learn

About three years go I became a foster parent, a single foster parent, to three young brothers ages 7, 8, and 10 years old. Over time two of them went into other foster homes, but one remains with me and has been with me from the outset. I've tried in that time to make expectations clear, while I have attempted to enable him to experience success in public school, in the community, on athletic teams, etc. It's been an interesting process.

One of the first times we went out to dinner – and I won't go to fast food places - I took them to O'Connor's in Worcester. One of them started eating the French fries off his plate with his hands and I said, "What are you doing?"

"I'm eating."

"I can see that. Use the fork."

"I'm eating French fries."

"I can see that too.

"You don't eat French fries with a fork," he says.

"Yes, you do - when they *give* you a fork. This isn't McDonald's."

Doesn't sound like much - right? But it was the beginning of establishing expectations and breaking old patterns of behavior.

Not long after that I took them to the Top of the Hub restaurant atop the Prudential Center in Boston, a rather elegant dining experience for which they were properly dressed if not totally prepared. Jay reached across the table and knocked over one of the foot high pieces of stemware on the beautifully appointed table. He looked over at me and said, "Charlie, this place is too good for us."

"No, it's not." I said.

I take him to church, which he hates, but he now knows you talk differently and behave differently in Church. For Christmas Mass, which is a bit longer than most weekly masses, we arrived early to ensure a seat. That made the event even longer than usual. Somewhere around the gospel he began to lose it. He leaned over and said to me, "this place would be a lot better if they had ice cream." I told him I'd pass on the suggestion to the pastor.

Kids learn by having new experiences and by having people believe in them and expect from them. One of the reasons I hate cry rooms in churches is because kids never learn that Church is different and that you're supposed to act and talk differently. By dispatching them to an isolated room, the momentary challenge they present is temporarily solved but the long-term effect of teaching respect and reverence is a lot longer in coming.

Kids have to know what we expect from them. That's not only true of behavioral expectations but also academic performance. Kids excel when people believe in them. That's what I have always found in Catholic education – the extra push, the commitment, the expectation that you're going to succeed.

It's Good for Kids

I've always seen it in Catholic schools and I see it at St. Mary School – and it's good for kids. Our kids are precious and we need to be conscious of that all the time. We need to invest all we can in them, love them, direct them, and do all we can to help them grow, mature, and succeed. We need to do what's good for them.

So that's really the answer to the question I posed at the outset and have already answered several times.

"Why Catholic education?"

Because it's good for kids. That's why.

Encouragement
Perkins School Recognition Day
June 18, 2005

Several years ago, when boys lived in the Manor, David was sitting in a chair in the front lobby directly across from the oil painting of our revered founder, the illustrious Dr. Franklin Perkins. This young man wasn't sitting there simply admiring the room's architecture as I recall. He had been asked to sit there to calm down a bit. I happen to come by, minding my own business as usual.

David pointed to the picture of Dr. Perkins, at that time in his life a distinguished, stately, and clearly elderly man probably in his 70's.

He said, "Who's that?"

In mock amazement, I said, "Who's *that*? That's the old, old Doc!"

David looks at the picture, looks back at me, and says, "Yeah, well it don't look like you."

This is the conclusion of our 109th year but, contrary to the nasty rumors, I haven't been here all that time. That doesn't mean I can't offer a hearty welcome to everyone here today. For each of the years I have been here, I've used my few minutes to reflect a bit on the past year but, more importantly, to concentrate on the future. However, I can't gloss over this past year without noting the great strides you all have made, which is why we're here today, and also point out that this was a year when one of our students published a book of his own poetry and one of our teachers all too suddenly passed away.

Usually in concentrating on the future, I've quoted famous figures who have left us little gems that I can mine for lessons and thoughts for us all. Those people have included Winston Churchill, who talked about the progression of events in time as having not only an end and a beginning of the end, but also an "end of the beginning." I've also cited Miss Piggy who offered the less-than-profound, but nonetheless practical bit of wisdom, "never eat more than you can lift." Today, however, I have neither sages to quote nor wisdom to bring from others. Rather I choose to relate to you a personal experience as a kid that I hope you will find helpful, if not truly enlightening.

When I was in elementary school in the eighth grade, we were given an assignment to write a composition. The teacher only gave as a guideline that we should write about "dinner time at my house." I thought for a while before I put pen to paper (there were no computers then!) and I then constructed an essay that was a mixture of humor, irreverence and satire.

Now, mind you, my teacher never said we had to do the traditional, boring, stupid, "every night at my house, mother and father and all the little Conroys sit down for a warm and friendly dinner full of sparkling conversation and wonderful culinary delights prepared by mother." No –

that would have given me the easy way out. I rather chose to do a lengthy essay on dinnertime at my house that was titled, "Come and Get it Before I Throw it Out!"

I expected and was even a bit disappointed when it raised no eyebrows from this eighth grade teacher, a nun. Now, I don't know what you know about nuns but most of them aren't known far and wide as being great joke crackers and humorists. In fact I think it's fair to say that they take a dim view of "class clowns." I wasn't trying to be a class clown. No one had to read this piece other than she and I.

I watched as she scanned it, sat down, read it more carefully, smiled and then totally cracked up. All modesty aside, I don't mind telling you this was one funny piece of literature. I had food flying around, milk being spilled, elbows and God-knows-what else on the table, and all sorts of odd things going on beneath the table as well. It wasn't pretty.

In no way did it truly reflect dinnertime in the Conroy household. It was merely meant to be funny, and it was, and my teacher was willing to acknowledge that. Sister Thomas said it was a creative, humorous piece even if it wasn't exactly what she had had in mind. It was certainly less traditional than all the other rote, run-of-the-mill drivel others turned in that she had to read. I was tremendously encouraged by that. She told me it was good. It was not what she expected – but it was good – and she liked it. In the process she may have created a monster.

I guess the fact that I'm talking about that 45 years after it happened says something. I felt her encouragement that I was doing something well even though strictly speaking it didn't fit the mold. She liked what I wrote and she wasn't afraid to tell me that. She found it entertaining. (As a side note, I had always plotted when the time came for an assignment on "How I Spent My Summer Vacation" to do a one-sentence paragraph: "I spent my summer vacation dreading the thought that I'd have to write an essay about "How I Spent My Summer Vacation." But the opportunity never came).

What's the point of it all? We all need words of encouragement and someone to say, "Good job. I like this. You did well." It's important that adults affirm for kids the things they do right. Sure, it's important that we let you know the stuff we don't like – and God knows we're good at that around here - but it's equally important to reinforce the stuff that they you *do* do right - just as Sister Thomas did for me.

One of my favorite stories involves two of baseballs legendary managers, Tommy Lasorda of the Dodgers and Sparky Anderson of the Cincinnati Reds. They were bitter rivals and fought for the National League championship year after year. Once during the playoffs LaSorda, who went to church pretty regularly, found himself on the morning of a big game in a small church with a few other people, one of whom was Sparky Anderson.

Never to be outdone, Tommy made sure he was just as devout as Sparky. When Sparky knelt to pray, Tommy knelt. When it came time to stand for the Gospel, Sparky jumped up, but Tommy did so just as fast. Sparky went up to communion and Tommy followed shortly after. When the service was over they both knelt down and then Sparky got up to leave. As he exited the church, he stopped, lit a candle, and walked out the door. LaSorda got up from his pew, walked over to the candle rack - and blew it out.

Of course that didn't in any way affect the intention that Sparky had when he lit the candle. I've said before and I'll say it again, *nobody* can blow out your candle try as they might. We should be doing everything we can to keep your candles burning by encouraging you – encouraging your creativity, your imagination, your ability to pay attention and learn. But you also have to work to keep your candle burning.

Encouragement is crucial. The secret to success as an adult is often that as a kid someone believed in you. I think it was Cornell social psychologist Urie Bronfenbrenner who once said that every kid needs to know that there is one adult who is absolutely wild about them. It's true but it's a two-way street. We have to believe in you and *you* have to believe in you.

South African bishop Desmond Tutu told a story at a commencement a few years back that I will paraphrase but try to maintain its true message. A farmer was standing in the barnyard one day feeding his chickens. A visitor came by and said to him, "hey, that one over there - that isn't a chicken."

"Sure he is," said the farmer. "Watch him. He goes along pecking like all the others."

"No," says the onlooker, "he's different. Look at his beak. Look at his huge wings. That's no chicken and, if you don't mind parting with one, give that one to me," said the visitor.

"Ok, what do I care," said the farmer

The visitor left with the bird, climbed a hill and, when the sun rose, he lifted the bird and launched it into the sky saying, "soar, eagle, soar."

The odd-looking bird spread its wings, was lifted by the wind, and flew off into the distance where it lived a wonderful and long life of freedom and independence, never again confined to a barnyard spending long days pecking at the ground.

We all have to be able to spread our wings and fly. We have to stop looking down at the ground and pecking the grain because it's been flung there and we're comfortable doing that and maybe know nothing better. We have to soar like the eagle and it's not good enough to just think we can - we have to *believe* we can.

To do that, we have to believe in ourselves. Sometimes we need a little help. We need someone to show us the way, to encourage us, to do what Sister Thomas did for me - and maybe even to lift us up and shove us up into the wind.

We may need a shoulder to lean on - but the shoulder is attached to the same arm that will push us off when the time comes - the same arm that will encourage us to soar like an eagle - not wander like a chicken.

People believe in you and we encourage you.

The rest is up to you.

Urges Goodbye to the Good Ole Days!
(Reprinted from *The Item*, Clinton, MA August 9, 2005)

"'Boy, take down your pants! No, no down to your ankles. And turn away from your sisters!'...

"Little wonder there was general titillation on the part of brothers and sisters. This really replaced sex education in the schools and was the first exposure...in more ways than one."

I'm guessing I'm not the only one who got a queasy feeling when I read those sentences in an *Item* (August 2) column titled "Double Punishment for School Misbehavior" by Frank Lepore. It was unclear whether the columnist was extolling the virtues of corporal punishment and possibly holding it out as a model to be revisited and adopted in our modern age or trying to get us to see the horror of child abuse. I still don't know what his purpose was - but I know what I think.

The piece correctly noted that parents who engaged in systematic physical abuse of children were often illiterate and couldn't understand the notes sent from school to home. They beat their children with straps ten times because they couldn't count beyond that. The author went on to point out that abuse on occasion was a by product of a father's "foul mood" and that "subjugation" of women in these kinds of violent households was a "common occurrence."

Not much to like here, right? So I want to conclude that the author was dead set against a modern repeat of this kind of behavior. If, as noted, little girls and little boys were first introduced to sex education through forced observation of abuse of their siblings, I'm going to suggest that that might easily have led to some distorted ideas about sex. Add that to the multiplicity of reasons not to beat children. As if we needed another.

Since the author didn't come down firmly on either side of the issue, here's what he should have said. Parents who engaged in brutal, corporal punishment of the type outlined were ignorant. Maybe they didn't know any better since physical abuse is multigenerational. Some parents simply didn't know any other way because we learn to parent from our parents. As noted, in some cases the violent paternal behavior toward children and maybe the wife was fueled by "rage," or a "foul mood," but it could have been from alcohol, or possibly undiagnosed or misunderstood mental illness. Often such beatings weren't about disciplining kids at all. They were about anger, familial discord, unrealized life expectations, or bitter career disappointments. Regardless of the cause, it was abuse clear and simple.

The subservient, obsequious attitude of parents of yesteryear when it came to ever questioning the clergy cannot be dismissed as a root cause of the horrible clerical abuse, uncovered years later, but which from reports was rampant in the 1950's and 60's. Witness how many priestly perpetrators could not be prosecuted because of their d relatively old ages or because of statutes of limitations that had run. Parents who knew sometimes did nothing. The scenario so graphically and disgustingly described in the *Item* column was all too often repeated in homes and schools all over.

One of my younger brothers came home from Catholic school one day and promptly displayed for my mother the marks on his posterior left by a 6th grade teacher who had beaten him with a pointer because of some classroom infraction. My mother, a formidable disciplinarian in her own right, but no respecter of those who abused children (especially hers), promptly rushed to school and confronted the principal who cavalierly dismissed the episode because the teacher "was having problems."

Not content to let it die there, my brother, not known far and wide for his modesty, went across the backyard of our Bronx home, dropped his pants, and showed the scars to my Uncle Andy, the deputy district attorney for Bronx County, who had spent his entire career prosecuting hard-bitten, nasty criminals. He too was appalled at what he saw.

What the teacher did was wrong and my mother confronted her supervisor about it. Some parents in those days not only abused their own kids but remained silent when others did and a lot more evil and heartache flowed from that kind of denial as well. The brother with the scarred buttocks displayed in a variety of venues went on to a stint in the U.S. Marine Corps and a successful career in law enforcement in and around New York City.

I don't want to prejudge the *Item* columnist's intent. I'm guessing that he was planning a second part to his column noting how the example in his first is really the paradigm for archaic, ignorant, inhumane treatment of children. I hope in that next column he will then go on to point out the need for all of us to be vigilant when it comes to protecting our children and other people's children.

I can tell you that, if a kid today comes to school with any kind of marks on him, people ask questions and then file a 51-A report with the Department of Social Services. Every teacher, social worker, nurse, physician, and school administrator in the Commonwealth is a "mandated reporter" and must report evidence of abuse to the authorities. Based on preliminary data and interviews, DSS and the county district attorney might pursue the matter further.

It really wasn't clear to me if *The Item* columnist was pining for "the good ole days" or was trying to get us to understand the horrors of child abuse in the "dark ages" of not so long ago by using such an horrific example. His purpose was vague. I do want to give him the benefit of the doubt.

I'm hoping it was the latter and that he was calling this episode to our attention to have us better understand the disgrace of it all. If, however, ie was waxing nostalgic about how kids were better controlled in a bygone era because of corporal punishment, he should know that anyone who tries it today will get a very different response from teachers, DSS, and the district attorney. That teacher who assaulted my brother would today lose her certification, be suspended immediately, possibly prosecuted, and then subjected to civil penalties as well.

Say good-bye to the good ole days. If it's nostalgia you're after - put a Sinatra or Patti Page LP on the record player, or play a rented video of "Casablanca" in black and white – but leave the kids alone. No one should ever force kids to remove their clothing and be beaten. If you do that you're a criminal - and these days that's just the way you'll be treated - whether you're a priest, a nun, a teacher - or a parent.

The good ole days weren't always so good.

They'll Remember How We Made Them Feel
Perkins Staff Awards Dinner
Manor Lawn
August 24, 2005

Multi-tasking, Successful Year

Some kids were on line for lunch in the cafeteria of a Catholic elementary school. As they made their way down the line, they noticed a printed sign next to a stack of big Red Delicious apples. It said, "Take just ONE. Remember God is watching." A little further down the line there was a huge plate of chocolate chip cookies. Next to the plate there was a hastily scrawled note on a napkin obviously written by one of the kids. It said: "Take as many as you want. God's watching the apples!"

I'm not going to speculate about the Almighty's oversight of either apples or cookies or ability to do two things at the same time. I suspect the latter is probably the case and that any Supreme Being worth his or her salt can easily undertake and successfully complete a variety of tasks simultaneously.

At Perkins we are also called on regularly to do a lot of different things, to do them well, and often to do them simultaneously. We were multi-tasking before it was fashionable. Every year I stand up here I have a lengthy litany of accomplishments to recite. That's true again this year.

This was a magnificent year. In addition to compiling a formidable record of academic success and clinical excellence, we this year opened a group home as evidence of our continuing effort to move further into community-based services. For those of you who haven't been around here for a fairly long time, you may not realize that this is our 2nd group home. Sixteen years ago we opened one for our adults on Chestnut Street in Clinton. We later sold that house, used the proceeds to help underwrite the construction of the Hymes Fitness Center in 1998, and then moved the adults to the brand new community-based apartments at Barlow.

Also this year we opened our Child and Adolescent Behavioral Health program, a group practice serving children and families from the community rather than Perkins students in the Farmer's Cottage on the north end of the campus. The program is also consulting to a number of public school districts concerning issues of kids with behavioral and mental health needs.

We opened the Academy for 11th and 12th graders in the modular units on Pinfeather Lane because of space needs. It has become not only an accepted, but valued, part of the program. It provides a somewhat separate, maybe even elite, environment for our older kids for whom our expectations about academic performance and behavior are quite high.

We added computers to all the classrooms at the Academy at the same time as we undertook a campus-wide project to increase computers in the residences for recreational and leisure use, the times kids really learn how to use them. I think it's astounding that we have 87 student computers for approximately 172 kids in our residential and day treatment programs. That's a formidable record that any school would be proud of. We also installed about 50 air conditioners this year so that the residences are as comfortable as our school buildings.

In the next few months in our latest initiative to serve the surrounding communities, you will see ground broken on a new child development/day care center on Creamery Road not too far from the Farmer's Cottage. The program will serve infants, toddlers and preschoolers and their families and I think will help us in our ongoing effort to position Perkins as the family-centered, strengths-based expert in child development and child welfare. The center will also build on the success of the parenting education program our clinicians inaugurated this past year.

All of these are tangible, easily recognizable examples of change, growth and improvement at a time when other agencies shrink, downsize, or contract their services. There may come a time when we are faced with similar decisions, but for the time being we continue to grow, to inaugurate new programs, and to expand our services into the community. That's pretty much what we've been doing for the last two decades.

Just an Old Habit?

The easy answer is that growth is an established Perkins pattern or habit and that old habits just die hard. Last month I had occasion to attend the quarterly treatment conference of one of the young men at Curtis Hall, for whom I have more than a passing interest, having been involved in his case and that of his brothers for about 4 years. At one point in the conference, this young man was told that discharge was around the corner, that a foster home was clearly on the horizon, but that he needed to put the finishing touches on his treatment here by refining his behavior especially working at being less rude to staff and peers.

This is no easy task for a guy who has a very quick tongue, colorful vocabulary, and an incisive, rapid fire verbal delivery. He was willing to consider the suggestion that he had to work on his impulsive tendency to be rude, but it was clear he saw it as a challenge. At one point he asked the team, "how long do I have to *not* be rude?" which I thought was a great admission of how difficult a task this might be for him.

While I certainly wasn't the only one in the room equipped to respond, I volunteered that it really wasn't a question of time-limiting his control over his rudeness but rather undertaking a behavioral change that might last (horror of horrors!) a lifetime. It wasn't a question of simply not being rude in order to "get out of Perkins," but rather changing one's behavior permanently. You could see that he viewed this as a formidable if not insurmountable task. Old habits do die hard.

I think our pattern of growth and diversification at Perkins is not just an old habit, however, like that old pair of shoes so nicely broken in or the comfort food we may love. I think rather that our growth represents an ongoing commitment to search for, if you'll let me coin an expression, "new and improved" ways of doing things. We simply assess where the gaps in service are and then successfully fill them. I think that's the pattern. We are good at doing it and it's just become the way we do business. It's not a habit at all. It's a commitment – and we do it well. <u>You</u> do it well. And - when I say "you," I mean all of you – all of us. Everyone here contributes whether it's through direct service to kids via teaching, counseling, supervision, meal preparation, or keeping the environment here so inviting and attractive that I continually get comments on the beauty of the campus and the upkeep of the buildings. Everyone here makes a significant contribution, although how we do it varies.

The Need Continues

And we'll keep on doing what we do because the need continues. While we are doing it we must keep in mind that the emphasis on reducing the number of kids in residential care has been renewed with more fervor than every before. At Perkins we have always felt that our services should be directed and calibrated to the kids who need them most, the most severely mentally ill and behaviorally disordered children.

The Governor's Commission on Children's Mental Health issued its final report this past July 1. The report included recommendations in 4 primary areas. It also made a number of detailed recommendations. Three of the primary area recommendations were:

1. Psychiatric hospitals and community based acute treatment programs, along with residential treatment facilities, such as intensive residential treatment programs, and behaviorally intensive residential treatment, play an important role in the continuum of care for children and adolescents; however, they should be the site of care only when therapeutically necessary; and only for as long as is therapeutically necessary.
2. Mental health care is health care.
3. With children and adolescents, identifying mental health problems early is vitally important, and when problems are identified, treatment must be readily available.

Some will look at those recommendations and become anxious. For us however, I think our response must be to accept the challenge, to acknowledge the validity of the initiatives, and to continue to advocate for the kids we serve knowing all the time that there are more of them than ever and that their conditions are more severe and acute than ever before.

The challenge for the policy-makers and implementers is to reduce services in an atmosphere of increasing need without abandoning those who most need service. We absolutely believe that mental health care is health care and that parity is a necessity. Our commitment to opening the child development center speaks volumes about our belief in early identification and treatment and services to the youngest children and their families.

We not only do not shrink from our responsibility to these children and their families, rather we continue to widen the continuum of services we offer. The group home on Center Bridge Road, the Child and Adolescent Behavioral Health program, and the Child Development Center are tangible evidence of our commitment to community-based, family-centered, strengths-based treatment.

A Bright Future

I am not certain that in the near future parts of our program will be downsized. That's always a possibility and, if the intent of the current Department of Social Services (DSS) initiative is realized, that's what might happen. I don't believe that reductions will happen evenly across the board or across the state. The stronger, better positioned, higher quality programs will suffer losses much less than programs which are marginal and which do not enjoy the support of DSS, school districts and families.

If there is a reduction in our residential program and it does have to downsize, what I foresee is that other parts of the program will upsize in response. Look at the example of day treatment that this year reached 70 kids in attendance. That's remarkable and a tribute to the day treatment and educational staffs. If the residential program does suffer reductions because of fewer admissions I think day treatment will continue to grow because the need is so great and because the pressure will still be on school districts to provide kids with the services that are outlined in their IEPs.

In some ways the future is uncertain, but for us even amid the uncertainty, I think the future is also bright. We are known far and wide as the best at what we do and I am confident that our well-deserved reputation for quality and adherence to standards will carry us through what some are predicting will be lean years. As long as we continue to serve the kids with the most severe needs, there will be demand for our services. The kids are not going away and, unlike other populations that have fewer rights and entitlements, kids with emotional, cognitive and behavioral needs have very well defined, court-tested rights to an education under both state and federal statutes. That's not likely to change.

If you're a special needs kid in state custody, you must be afforded the same educational opportunities as your counterpart who lives with his or her family. If you have an IEP and it says you need specialized services including residential or day treatment services, it is a violation of state and federal law to deny that to you regardless of how much money is available to fund it. That's the way it is. As Casey Stengel, the old manager of the 26-time world champion New York Yankees once said, "you could look it up!"

Our commitment to kids must remain on both the advocacy and direct service levels. We must continue to voice our opposition to any reduction in services to kids who need them and are entitled to them. At the same time we must continue to upgrade our services and to provide them in ways that improve the lives of children while they're here and after they leave. We must help them to live better lives and, hopefully, help them to live happier lives as well.

A recent opinion column in the *New York Times* on August 16, 2005 made the point that, finally, we may be coming to the widespread realization that social and emotional learning and academics do not proceed along parallel lines that do not intersect. In fact the authors report that, as a result of an analysis of over 300 research studies, "social and emotional learning programs significantly improve students academic performance." We have known this for a long time and I think we would echo the conclusion of the authors: "that children who are given clear behavioral standards and social skills allowing them to feel safe, valued, confident and challenged, will exhibit better school behavior and learn more to boot."

We've never viewed this as rocket science but it's nice to have it confirmed by a review of the professional research. Clear behavioral expectations and social and emotional growth are directly related to academic success. Kids grow intellectually not purely on the basis of classroom instruction but also as a result of the development of their own social and emotional skills. The experience kids have at Perkins benefits them not only while at Perkins but for years to come.

Childhood Experiences

Years from now kids will remember their experiences here. Even as adults they will be a product, as we all are, of our formative years. Several years ago there was a popular film titled, *Antwone Fisher*, in which a starring role was played by Denzel Washington. The film exemplified how our childhood experiences and how people make us feel get carried into our adult years. Our COO, Laura Beckman-Devik, used the video in a training about a year and a half ago and at that time I lent her Fisher's autobiography. Antwone had some horrific experiences of physical and sexual abuse in foster care and, as an adult in his poem, "Who Will Cry for the Little Boy," he still asked:

> Who will cry for the little boy, lost and all alone?
> Who will cry for the little boy, abandoned without his own?
> Who will cry for the little boy? He cried himself to sleep.
> Who will cry for the little boy? He never had for keeps.
> Who will cry for the little boy? He walked the burning sand.
> Who will cry for the little boy? The boy inside the man.
> Who will cry for the little boy? Who knows well hurt and pain.

Who will cry for the little boy? He died and died again.
Who will cry for the little boy? A good boy he tried to be.
Who will cry for the little boy, who cries inside of me?"

As adults we still think of our childhood experiences good and bad since they form a part of who we are. Last week I was walking up from school back to the Manor. I was on the walk between Memorial and Wyman when I heard a young voice coming from the parking lot of Hermann.

"Hello, Dr. Conroy!" he said. I thought it was Tyler but thought maybe it was Saul, or maybe even Dmitri from Pappas, since they always say hello to me. But I couldn't distinguish from the distance who exactly it was. So, I asked, "who's that?"

The response was simple, but wonderful at the same time, because it told me that, whoever he was, he believed I recognized him and knew him as a person. He didn't have to know that the combination of middle age eyesight and/or memory loss was causing a momentary lapse in identifying him. What followed was a response that I repeated to Laura, Doug and Kerry when I got back to the office for our Executive Team meeting. To my question, "who's that?" came a great answer. He shouted back, "It's ME!"

I love that response because it suggests that he expected that I would know who he was, even if at that moment I didn't. He had the confidence to think I did and that's what's important. He felt acknowledged and he felt important.

"I've Never Seen Him Smile Before"

I had an interesting experience in the early part of the summer. I had my class of graduate students from Fitchburg State here to do a strategic planning simulation in the library at Janeway. We were scheduled to start around 3pm and some of our Perkins students were still in the building, mostly kids in the after school program. One of my graduate students arrived and I was walking her down to the library. We had just gone past the rotunda.

She's a teacher in a local school district not too far from here. She mentioned that the team in her district had referred one of her students here and he was currently enrolled. As fate would have it, that same kid, a teenager, came around the corner from the dining room and was walking down the hallway. He was walking directly at us but was in such animated, light-hearted conversation with a friend that he never noticed us at all.

I didn't think much of it. I get ignored all the time. However, his former teacher did notice something. As we continued walking to the library, she stopped, turned around to look at the kid who just passed, then turned to me and said, "I've never seen him smile before."

There's a lot of great things that go on around here and I've enumerated some of this past year's accomplishments already. However I have to tell you that, while I'm exceedingly proud of our academic, clinical, and residential programs, and while I'm delighted we have been able to open new programs like Child and Adolescent Behavioral Health, the Academy, and Center Bridge Hall, and while I'm very excited by the prospect of constructing and opening a new child development center, there's something else that I am even more elated about.

Of all the things I've talked about and of which we are proud I think most of all I am pleased that this past year we succeeded in putting a smile on the face of a kid who according to his own teacher never smiled before. Of all the things we do that's among the most significant because it tells me we're doing what we set out to do.

We are educating that young man, we are treating him with dignity, we are providing him with the skills he needs to succeed but – you know what? – we're doing something else too. We are enabling him to have something it sounds like he's never experienced before – some degree of happiness – and for that I am indebted to all of you.

It's important to have a great curriculum. It's important to have great facilities and wonderful buildings. It's important to have great, well-coordinated, quality programs. But managing to put a smile on the face of kid who never smiled before overshadows all the other accomplishments because it's a great gauge of how much we care and how well we do what we do.

They'll Remember How We Made Them Feel

Poet Maya Angelou said it best: "I've learned that people will forget what you said, people will forget what you did, but people will never forget how you made them feel." She's right.

When kids leave here, I suspect that they will not remember everything we taught them and all their academic accomplishments, but they'll remember how we made them feel.

They may not remember how well they were directed, supervised and guided, but they'll remember how we made them feel.

They may not remember the great facility and wonderful environment, but they'll remember how we made them feel.

They may not remember the quality of our school and clinical programs, but they'll remember how we made them feel.

Perhaps they may even remember that it was here that they first *began* to feel, to get beyond past episodes of depression, of profound disappointment, or histories of abuse or neglect.

Maybe - they'll even remember - that this was the place where they were first able to smile.

Administrators Need to Use Their Brains
(Reprinted from *The Item*, Clinton MA February 14, 2006)

Just when you thought it was safe to send your kids back to school, that band of clueless school administrators, who defend their disciplinary actions by pointing to misguided policies designed solely to cover themselves, is back with renewed vigor. A six-year-old was suspended in Brockton recently for touching the waistband of a classmate, apparently with two fingers touching her skin. The principal suspended him and quickly pointed to a school "sexual harassment" policy. Again I ask: "What do these people use for brains?"

We've had little kids – six-, seven-, eight-year olds kids, disciplined in school, sometimes by means of expulsion or suspension, for threatening to "kill" classmates with whom they had a disagreement over candy. We've seen young kids suspended for taking water pistols to class because a school policy prohibited "guns." Mindless school administrators, conscious only of personal interest and counseled by school attorneys not averse to lucrative litigation, have brought us to the point where children's interests are threatened.

This is stupid. Whatever happened to school administrators who looked out for kids, counseled them, talked to parents, and worked closely with law enforcement while reminding them that kids have rights too? What was this Brockton principal thinking about, other than her own career, when she suspended this little boy for "sexual harassment," the meaning of which is a mystery to him?

The principal should resign, the Superintendent who's defending her should resign, and, if the school committee who hires the latter, who then hires the former, doesn't take action, *they* too should resign or be swiftly recalled by parents and irate citizens who know this craziness has gone much too far.

I teach in a graduate program that prepares principals and other administrators for service in our schools. If any one of them ever turned in a paper using this situation as a case study and suggested acting as this principal did, he or she would soon know the meaning of grade deflation. It's totally unacceptable. Administrators should use their heads. Policy is important - but so is compassion and administrative discretion. We pay them to use their heads, not to point to a page in a policy manual to defend the indefensible.

Six-year-olds are incapable of sexual harassment. They don't know what it is and, consequently, I don't think they can commit it. They might engage in sexually inappropriate play, rough play, even aggressive play – but they probably don't understand the implications of it. Adults need to tell them and not simply take action to discipline them. Whatever happened to capitalizing on a "teaching moment?" Surely this was one.

Sexual harassment was originally a "workplace" concept (remember Clarence Thomas?). It has now been extended to colleges and high schools. In those venues, adolescents and adults unfortunately use sex for leverage or intimidation purposes and it is wise to extend sexual harassment policies to those school levels. But to first and second grade? Please!

"Quid pro quo" harassment ("I'll promote you if you...") or "hostile environment" harassment (creating or maintaining an atmosphere that is pervasively sexually demeaning) hardly seems to apply in this case. The 6-year-old did not engage in "repeated" instances of harassment, a usual definition found in policies. He was neither in a position to professionally harm his peer nor did he create a pervasive atmosphere of harassment. I'm not sure he did anything but be a 6-year-old - an insensitive 6-year old to be sure - but a 6-year old nonetheless.

Because some school district has panicked and promulgated a policy written by a lawyer with a slow practice and equally slow intellect doesn't mean this kid committed a crime or even an infraction that merits suspension from school. What ever happened to sitting down a 6-year-old and telling him that's not the way to play? Did principals forget how to do that? The kid isn't exposing himself or forcing someone to commit a sex act, the kind of incidents that absolutely should get a school administrator's attention.

The kid grabbed a classmate by her pants top - for God's sake! And these administrators, intent on self-protection, suspend him? What a disgrace! Educators are supposed to educate and nurture kids. This principal is incapable of either.

The time has come for parents to say, "Enough is enough." This little boy didn't do anything that in a moment of play, excitement, or explosion of energy, a lot of other little boys haven't done. Despite what his principal thinks, he's not a pervert or sexual harasser. He's a 6-year old boy.

She should know that. She should do everyone a favor and find other work because she's not very good at this job.

The Wrong Way to Reform Child Welfare
(Reprinted from *The Boston Globe*, February 25, 2006)

"They didn't tear down the Central Artery before building the tunnel." This comment, about everyone's favorite public works project, was made by a colleague who, like me, is the CEO of a child welfare agency that offers residential treatment to severely abused and disturbed children. He was comparing the Big Dig with the massive restructuring of child welfare now underway in Massachusetts, and his message was simple: Don't destroy the infrastructure that is out there before you have a better one to replace it.

Those responsible for complex government agencies are, of course, mindful of public perceptions. So when initiating change, they try to proceed at the right pace. Moving too slowly can make change appear tentative and lacking in clear purpose, perceptions that can actually compromise its success. Moving too quickly can make the process seem impulsive, risky, and heedless of potential dangers.

It would be nice to say that the present restructuring is going at just the right speed, but it is not. Following discussions with providers of foster care, residential treatment, and community-based mental health services, the Department of Social Services (DSS) is now rushing to transform in months a system that has been in place for decades. By summer the "Family Networks" system will be inaugurated, and strong efforts will be underway to reduce reliance on residential schools and group homes, and increase dependence on intensive foster care and community services for children in need.

It is difficult to quibble with the philosophy driving this restructuring. It is rooted in some sound child welfare thinking. The prologue to the DSS document soliciting responses from potential providers, shares one of the agency's goals: "We believe that we must align the child welfare system to dramatically increase the proportion of children who maintain or achieve a permanent family or other lifelong connection, with the support and guidance of the child welfare system."

Who would dispute that children are better off in biological or foster homes than in congregate living situations? Who would argue that the child welfare system should not be as "child-focused," "family-centered," and "community-based" as possible, or that it should not capitalize on the strengths of families rather than their weaknesses? And in more cold-blooded terms, who would not like to see cuts in "costly" residential care?

The only real argument against any of these fine principles is that the tunnel is not yet built. In its haste to dismantle the existing system, DSS is ignoring the needs of the most deeply hurt and troubled children and adolescents. There will always be a small proportion of young people who need intensive care in a secure, safe, clinically rich residential placement, owing to the horrors they have experienced and the damage that has been done to their bodies, minds, and spirits.

The DSS cannot help but be aware of such cases. Indeed, the department argued in favor of a residential placement for Haleigh Poutre, and because that argument did not prevail, DSS had to deal with the truly horrific results. Had DSS been able to place Haleigh in a residential program, she would not have ended up on life support, and the department would not have become mired in the bitter question of its removal.

In a comprehensive residential treatment environment the process of sorting out whether Haleigh's injuries were self-inflicted or the product of abuse by adults might have begun. More significantly, healing would have begun. A child who had experienced more misery than any child should bear could have experienced some respite from whatever or whomever had been torturing her. She could then have begun the course of treatment needed "to achieve a permanent family or other lifelong connection." That step just needed to happen.

Residential treatment provides a safe, secure, and nurturing environment for children who need it most. At the moment and for the foreseeable future, comparable services are simply not available in most community-based settings regardless of the euphemisms or professional jargon employed to suggest otherwise.

Severely abused, neglected, and mentally ill children need intensive care, treatment, and therapy to recover. For the moment and the foreseeable future, there exists neither an adequate system of community-based mental health services nor a cadre of trained foster parents to serve these young people. To assert otherwise is to deny what we all see every day.

Your World, Your Community, and You.
Clinton High School National Honor Society
Chocksett Inn, Sterling, MA
May 2, 2006

Your World: The Last 18 Years

What I hope to do this evening is to take a look at how the world has changed in your brief lifetimes, review some of the recent thinking on how it continues to change, and then speculate a bit about what it all means. Finally, I would like to look at some of the constants in our lives-those things that anchor us, sustain us, and keep us balanced in a world that is undergoing such radical transformation. I'm talking about things like community, character, values, and parents. The decisions we make in regard to each of those are as important as those relating to changes in the world in which we live.

Before we do that, let's drop back a bit and see how some of life's events have unfolded these last 18 or so years. Many of you were born in 1988 and the younger members of this senior class, in 1989. In 1988, the winter Olympics were held in Calgary, Alberta, Canada and the summer Olympics in Seoul, South Korea. That same year George Herbert Walker Bush, the father of the current President, was himself elected to the country's highest office in an election that pitted him against Massachusetts Democratic Governor Michael Dukakis.

In 1988, NASA resumed space flights following the Challenger disaster in January 1986. In December of that year Pan American Flight 103 exploded over Lockerbie, Scotland. It was the work of Libyan terrorists and was a harbinger of things to come.

In June 1989, the government of the People's Republic of China brutally put down student protestors in Tiananmen Square. In November of that year, Douglas Wilder and David Dinkins were elected Governor of the Commonwealth of Virginia and Mayor of the City of New York respectively, becoming the first two African-Americans to hold those offices. In December 1989, a new television show, *The Simpsons,* had its television premiere.

By the time you were entering first grade, six years later in 1994, Bill Clinton had been in the White House over a year and a half. One of his predecessors, Richard Nixon, died that same year, 20 years after resigning the Presidency in disgrace over the Watergate scandal. In May of that same year Nelson Mandela became the first black President of South Africa and the next month, June, O. J. Simpson led the police on a now famous car chase. There was no World Series that year; it was cancelled due to a players' strike. The Red Sox would have to wait another ten years before winning a World Series, but their fans were used to waiting.

In 1995, when the younger members of this senior class turned six years old, the Murrah Federal Office Building in Oklahoma City was bombed by American terrorists killing 168 people, many of them children in a day care center housed in the building. In October, ten people were found guilty in the first bombing of the World Trade Center, two years before in 1993. In 1999, when you were either ten or eleven years old, two students at Columbine High School in Littleton, Colorado, massacred their fellow students and teachers.

In 2001, in the fall of your last year of Middle School on a day none of us will ever forget, New York City and the Pentagon were attacked and a plane was crashed into the hills of Western Pennsylvania, all the work of terrorists. In 2004, the Red Sox finally won an American League pennant and, ultimately, the World Series. In the case of the Trade Center and Pentagon bombings, we all hope that we will never witness anything like it again. In the case of the Red Sox, I can pretty much *assure* you that you will never see anything like that again.

Our World – Flat?

But, as they say, that was all then, and this is *now*. We live in this new century and new millennium in a world that is radically different from what it was just ten years ago. We got through Y2K without too much chaos and now face the possibility of a global bird flu pandemic. The technological explosion that your generation pretty much grew up with has forever changed life on this planet.

Last year in a book titled *The World is Flat,* that worked its way up to the top of the best seller lists, *New York Times* correspondent Tom Friedman developed an interesting idea. Friedman believes that, largely as a result of technology, the world's commercial and information playing fields have been leveled or, as he puts it, the world has been "flattened."

Communication is instantaneous, accurate, and clear and that has revolutionized the way we interact, do business, and live generally. Computer software and a fiber-optic network that spans the globe have made it possible to outsource a variety of jobs that before were done in America, including such routine things at tax return preparation. Friedman notes that in 2005, 400,000 American tax returns are expected to be completed in India. Accountants in America will focus on more specialized customer-friendly work such as financial planning and counseling and outsource the "grunt work" of tax prep to Indians who have been trained to do it.

Did you know that American hospitals and radiologists outsource the reading of CAT scans and MRIs to India and even Australia? An MRI or CAT scan done in the evening in the United States in a small community hospital can be transmitted to India that night, read, and deciphered. A full report can be completed and on the American radiologist's desk in the morning because, when it's nighttime here, it's day time there. Amazing.

He points out that there are McDonald's where, when you put your order in at the drive-through speaker, it's actually being handled at a communications center hundreds or maybe thousands of miles away. The communications people talk to the customer, take a snapshot, put the order up on the screen, and transmit the order to the food prep people back at the same McDonald's where the customer is. In the process they have actually cut order time.

Friedman says that, "You have to constantly upgrade your skills. There will be plenty of good jobs out there in the flat world for people with the knowledge and ideas to seize them." He counsels his own kids not to finish their dinner, as he was told as a child, "because people in China and India are starving," but rather to finish their homework "because people in China and India are starving for your jobs."

He tells parents to "turn off the television, put away the iPod, and get your kids down to work." He notes that the students who make it to the California Institute of Technology, or Caltech, are kids who come from public schools rather than private schools and he quotes the president of that great scientific university who says that, "I look at the kids who come to Caltech, and they grew up in families that encouraged them to work hard and to put off a little bit of gratification for the future and to understand that they need to hone their skills to play an important role in the world."

The long and short of it is that you need to expand your technological skills *while* you improve your personal and interpersonal skills and - this is the bottom line - work hard *now* to get something that's worthwhile later on. The fact that you're here tonight tells me that I may be preaching to the choir, since you're already off to a good start.

I was very encouraged to hear that the Caltech president gives public schools their due. Whether you know it or not, but I suspect you do, you have had the good fortune to grow up and be educated in a community which values education and which supports its public schools at great cost to its citizens. I know of no other town in this region that has consistently supported public education the way Clinton does. Look at the resources, the physical plant, the athletic fields, and the dedication and longevity of the teaching staff and administration. There's a certain magic here that a lot of towns would do well to emulate. The fact that the Rotary hosts this gathering every year is also a clear indication of the community's emphasis on and commitment to education.

You have been fortunate, and I know you are grateful. I repeat to you tonight what I said to the graduating class of Clinton High School 15 years ago. "Qui multum datum est, multum quaeretur ab eo," "to whom much is given, much is expected." This community has given you a lot, your parents have given you a lot, and we all want you to succeed.

Community

Family and community are important parts of our upbringing, who we are, and who we hope to be. When I was growing up in New York City, neighborhoods were often ethnically based, which has helped to give me a great appreciation for diversity and the strengths of particular ethnic groups.

I've always thought that the Italian community had the corner on the family and community market. Italians love family. They love gathering around meals to be with family and they emphasize the centrality of family and *community*. I've always admired them for that.

I moved up to Massachusetts in 1987 and, while I left most of my family in New York, little by little, they moved out of the city but stayed in the vicinity - in Westchester, Rockland, or Orange County not too far away.

So, in the first ten years when I did go back to visit New York relatives, I really didn't go to the city itself. It wasn't until my younger daughter started as a freshman at Fordham University in 1997 that I began to go back to the city where I grew up. I was especially fond of a neighborhood not too far from Fordham that we knew as Arthur Avenue, or "Little Italy," when I attended Fordham in the late 1960's.

Arthur Avenue is sort of an ethnic Italian enclave not unlike the North End in Boston. When we were living in the Bronx and my girls were young, a few weekends a month we went over to "Little Italy" usually as a follow up to a visit to the nearby Bronx Zoo. On the way back from the zoo we would stop and I'd load up on the best bread, sausage, pasta, and ravioli there is.

One store, that specialized in fresh pasta made right before your eyes, was run by an older couple, Lilly and Mario Borgatti, and I got my stuff there every week. I hadn't been back there in *ten* years. When I walked in, I saw a big picture of Lilly, and I knew right away she must have passed away. When it was my turn at the counter, I stepped up. Mario was waiting on another customer. He turned to me like I had been there last week and said. "So, how ya doin'? How ya been?" Ten years pass-and it's like you never left.

On another trip I asked Tony, the guy in the deli, to wrap the parmigiano cheese and the sausage up well because I had a four-hour ride ahead of me.

"Where ya goin'?" he said.

"I'm going to Massachusetts," I said. I usually say, "not too far from Boston," because no one's ever heard of Lancaster.

"Boston!" he says. "I was up dere last year."

"Really," I said.

"Yeah," he says, "I had dinner in a great restaurant and, when we got done, da waiter comes over with a big empty bottle o' wine with little numbers in it and shakes it. If ya get the number dat matches ya table, ya get dinner for free."

"Yeah," I said, "that's Vinnie Testa's."

Tony looks at me and screams, "How d'you know dat?"

I start to tell him that Vinnie's is a chain, but he's already calling the guy at the other end of the counter.

"Patsy, c'mon over here." "Dis here guy was in da same restaurant wit me when I was in Boston. Remember da one I told ya bout where dey shake da bottle and give ya da free dinner?"

He goes on regaling Patsy with the story. By the time he finished, even I was ready to swear we were there at the same time. If I stayed long enough, he would have convinced me we were at the same table.

The point again is *community*. The pasta storeowner remembered me after ten years and the deli guy immediately connected and identified with me. It's those kinds of connections that make a community, and you're fortunate to live in a town that is truly a community.

When people ask you where you're from, smile, speak right up, and say you're from Clinton - and say it in a way that shows you're proud, because you should be. This is not your basic antiseptic, vanilla, Wonder bread town like so many others. This town has a distinct character and identity. Yes, politics is a contact sport and debate is ongoing, but it's a town with a proud history and an especially good record of taking care of its kids and schools.

Know Who You Are

So, I guess you have to carry on the legacy. A lot has been given to you and we expect that you will be successful adults and, when the time comes, good parents. There's no denying that academic preparation and technological expertise help to ensure success in our world, but personal characteristics, family, community and values are equally important. You have to know who you are.

Francisco Alarcon is a poet in California who has a wonderful way of getting his message across. He writes in Spanish and succinctly says what few others are able to. One of his poems is titled, "De Amor Oscuro," "Of Dark Love":

>dos caminos hay en el mundo: el verse
>un dia en un espejo o el nunca llegar
>a verse de veras, verse es vivir,
>no verse, estar muerto

>there are two ways in the world: to see
>yourself one day in the mirror, or never see
>your true self-image, to see yourself is to live,
>not seeing yourself is death

You have to know who you are before you know what you want to be. One follows the other. The Stoic philosopher Epictetus said, "First say to yourself what you would be; and then do what you have to do." We live in a world where it's almost not a joke anymore to believe that old wisecrack that life is all about, "whoever has the most toys wins." BMWs, McMansions, and showy possessions have their place, but they're really not what matters.

Character, values, honesty, decency, respect for others, and watching out for the little guy-they're what matters. Dedication to family, devotion to others, community service, and respect in the community still trump flashy cars and huge houses. You were raised in a town where people have understood that for a long time.

Work hard and try to get ahead and do it in an honest way and take care of the people in your life along the way. You've heard that no one on their deathbed has ever said, "I should have spent more time at the office." William Sloane Coffin, the 1960's antiwar activist at Yale and minister at Riverside Church in New York, who recently passed away, said that, "even if you win the rat race, you're still a rat." There's some truth to that.

In Your Hands

There's an old story about a smart young man in ancient times who wanted to be known as the most brilliant in his country and, thus, be recognized as a sage, the person with the greatest reputation for wisdom. To do that he had to replace the current sage, an elderly but very wise man. The younger man had devised a plan, actually a trick, to fool the old man. If he could do so, it would mean that the young man would himself become a sage. He just had to fool him.

The young man decided that he would confront the old sage while holding a live sparrow in his hands behind his back and ask the simple question, "Is the bird in my hands alive or is it dead?" If the old sage said the bird was alive, the young man could simply snap its neck and show the old man the lifeless corpse thereby proving him wrong. If he said the bird was dead, the young man would simply bring his hands forward, open them, and let the bird fly off, also showing that the sage was wrong.

The young man approached the old sage with the bird behind his back and asked the question, "Is the bird in my hands alive or dead?"

The old sage thought for a second. The young man again questioned him. "Is the bird in my hands alive or dead?"

The sage stared deeply into the eyes of his young challenger and slowly responded. "The answer," he said, "is in *your* hands."

You have been offered great opportunities, and you are taking advantage of what's been offered. The answer, your future, is ultimately in *your* hands.

You are learning to balance academic and societal demands with the demands of morality and character, emphasizing what's right and decent and good. A lot of what you have learned and who you are becoming is because of the adults around you. Some of those adults are your parents who share in your accomplishments tonight and who will share in more of them in the future. Tell them that you appreciate not only what they have done but also what they will continue to do for you. And - when you do that - don't be afraid to tell them that you love them. In Clinton, where people have no problem speaking their mind, show your Clinton roots, and tell your parents that you love them. Some people never get around to doing that and it's unfortunate.

Pete Hamill, a quintessential New York journalist, often writes of life in my hometown. I read a piece years ago that I shared with that same Clinton High School graduating class of 1991, 15 years ago. Hamill talked about his father and the need for us to know who loves us. Kids need to know it, but parents need to know it too.

He writes of his father:

…I didn't really know him; he left school at twelve to work as a stonemason's apprentice and had struggled for a while at night school…But he really didn't know how to deal with me…he was still Irish and I was an American. I loved the way he talked and the way he stood on the corner with a fedora and raincoat on Sunday mornings, an Irish dude waiting for the bars to open, and I loved the way he once hit a guy with a ball bat because he insulted my mother. I just never knew if he loved me back.

That's my final suggestion to you this evening. Let those who love you know that you love them back. Do it. Nobody else can.

What did the sage say? The answer is in *your* hands.

"It's Never Too Late To Be What You Might Have Been."
Perkins School Recognition Day
June 17, 2006

Good morning and welcome to the Recognition Day ceremony marking the conclusion of the 110th year of the Perkins School.

Every Monday *The New York Times* publishes a section called *Metropolitan Diary*, a collection of short clips about life in the city. Recently someone wrote in and told of a conversation between an adult and a young child as they approached an ice cream stand on a sidewalk in Manhattan.

"Can I have an ice pop?" asks the little girl.

"Yes – and what's the magic word?" prompts the woman.

The little girl thinks for a second and says, "Abracadabra?"

Why is that humorous? It's funny because it's not expected. The woman is trying to get the little girl to say, "please," but what she gets is a reasonable, but totally unexpected, answer.

Life can be like that. We can end up dealing with the unexpected, with the cards we're dealt, or with the way things are rather than the way we would like them to be. Few of you probably ever thought you would attend Perkins School but, for whatever reason, you're here and, of course the staff and I are quite happy about that. It may have been unexpected, but it's worked out rather well – for you and for us. There's nothing worse than having a school with no kids.

Life really is about dealing with the unexpected. While much of what occurs in life is predictable, planned, and by design, some of it is unpredictable, serendipitous (look that one up!) and to a large degree unexpected. We have to be resilient, flexible, even courageous to deal with the unexpected. People who can do that, succeed. Those who can't, struggle in life.

Some of you have had unexpected losses or disappointments. In some cases you have had more of that than many of the adults here today. However, you have managed to begin the process of surmounting the challenges and obstacles in your way. That will help you later on in life. We all have disappointments from time to time. It's how you deal with them and learn from them that counts.

It's never too late to rise above the challenges and disappointments. The author George Eliot, who despite the pen name was a woman, said, "It's never too late to be what you might have been." That's a great sentiment. "It's never too late to be what you might have been." There's always tomorrow. It just takes courage.

It takes courage to pick up the pieces and move on when life has dealt you a blow that hurts, that disappoints, that knocks you down. Courage is not something we often associate with kids since we have this idea that it's synonymous with being a hero, but it's not. Courage, particularly the courage to move on with your life, comes in many forms and it's just as evident in kids as it is in adults.

Each year *The Boston Globe* prints essays of 6th graders in the Boston Public Schools who write on the topic of courage. The paragraphs they write show amazing insight and understanding of what it means to be courageous even when it happens in modest, everyday circumstances.

One 6th grader, Yeison Quinceno, wrote about how he showed courage when he helped a classmate, Carlos, who most of the kids didn't like. He became his class partner. He writes:

> "When I came to his desk he was quiet, and about 30 seconds later he asked, 'So how do we start?' I opened my notebook and I told him, 'Copy what's on the board.' He did the exact things I told him to do, which really surprised me.
>
> "His head went down again, and he asked, 'Why didn't anyone decide to help me?' That also surprised me, and I said, 'If you stop bothering everyone else, I'm sure they would help you.' From that day we became friends, and he didn't bother anybody anymore."

Yeison concludes:

> "This really made the difference. Carlos became a much nicer person, and I also changed. That day I felt courageous and I realized that one small kindness could make a huge difference. This showed me that I can be courageous and can make a lot of changes."

What Yeison did took courage. No one else was willing to help Carlos. He took the risk that the other kids might make fun of him for doing it, but he did it anyway. Courage is not something just found on a battlefield, or in a burning building, or in some kind of huge crisis. There is everyday courage and kids have it as much as adults.

We need everyday courage to face and overcome the challenges, disappointments, and unexpected obstacles in life. We have to confront them, get past them, and move on with our lives to achieve success. Saying it, of course, is much easier than doing it, and I know that, but it's true nonetheless. The unexpected barriers and obstacles that are thrown in our way in life can become the steppingstones for our success. We just need the courage to get past what's in our way.

It's been said that, "if it doesn't kill you, it makes you stronger" and there may be some truth to that. If you can learn to deal with challenges and obstacles as a kid, you enter your adult years much better prepared than someone who has slid through life with no barriers to overcome. Surely as an adult there will be additional challenges and, never having confronted any as a child, can put someone at a real disadvantage.

So – what does it all mean?

It means that having challenges in your lives, even ones much greater than other kids your age, might in the long run prepare you to be better adults, parents, and human beings. It doesn't mean that you can't go on to achieve lasting success. Quite the contrary, it may help you attain success. You just need the courage to move beyond what's in your way.

There's still time. It takes courage - and you have it. We see it within you every day. Success in life is about having the courage to face and overcome the unexpected.

"It's never too late to be what you might have been."

Perseverance, Risk-Taking, and Building Bridges
Perkins Staff Awards Dinner
Manor Lawn
August 23, 2006

Questions

As I was writing this someone was looking over my shoulder at one point and said, "How long is that talk going to be?"

I answered, "I figure about 20 or 25 minutes, Jay."

"Yeah," he says. "And you say *I* talk too much."

Two weeks ago in the *Boston Globe* Dan Shaugnessy, the paper's very talented sports writer, told of a visit he had to Boston Red Sox owner John Henry's home. Shaugnessy questioned Henry about some past comments he made about leadership.

"I ask him if he regrets sitting before Red Sox Nation in the hours after Theo Epstein resigned and telling us he questioned whether he was fit to be owner of the Red Sox."

"Henry responded, 'One of the things that happens in the position of leadership is the people seldom see anyone question themselves publicly. One of the things that can be wrong with leadership is if you don't question yourself. If something happens that you consider a large negative, don't you think it's healthy to question yourself?'"

I don't generally take a lot of advice from Red Sox owners, managers, players or fans. However, even a team that wins once every 86 years can have something to offer occasionally and I think Mr. Henry's observations are right on target. I've been doing a lot of questioning lately about the results of this year, the general trends in the state regarding the work we do, and our stated plans for the future.

Some of the questioning must be about me, as John Henry suggests, given the fact that we lost $600,000 this year in an environment hardly friendly to our "bread and butter" services, residential treatment. For that I take full responsibility. For the moment, however, my misgivings pale in comparison to a larger issue - what it all means for this organization in the future.

Right now, we all labor under a salary freeze, but I am confident that it will be lifted given our latest performance and positive admissions data. I think it says something that, in this constricted, anti-residential environment, professionals and parents continue to express their confidence in Perkins by making referrals. But there still must be some questioning about the organization itself, its place and role in the larger scheme of things, and where we see ourselves in the years to come.

Some of that will be taken up when we begin our strategic planning process again this year, but it's not premature to ask some questions now.

The questions include: Where are we? Where are we going? And how will we fit into the larger picture in the future?

Hostile Environment

I think we must search for answers to those questions in the context of this hostile environment, one not just averse to residential treatment but, I think, in which there is a growing distaste for programs that help vulnerable people, even children. That search for answers will help us to develop some strategies for the future.

Last week the Governor of Massachusetts vetoed legislation that would have provided universal preschool to children across the Commonwealth. This happened despite what many believe is incontrovertible evidence that preschool education has long-term beneficial effects on children. An op-ed piece in the *Boston Globe* cited among those benefits the following:

"Children who go to quality preschool are: more likely to become good readers in elementary school; less likely to be placed in special education or held back a grade; more likely to graduate from high school and attend college; (and) less likely to need public assistance as adults."

How do you ignore that and veto a bill that would provide services to preschoolers? How do you do that in a federally mandated *No Child Left Behind*/Massachusetts Education Reform environment that ostensibly is focused on improving student performance? You want performance, you want improvement in test scores, but you ignore the research that informs you about how to get kids there? How does that make sense?

The lack of quality, affordable child care and preschool education disproportionately affects the children of the poor and families where both parents must work. These children will arrive at school disadvantaged compared to their counterparts from families who can afford childcare and preschool. How do you veto a law like that?

Sounds incongruous doesn't it? It's like dismantling a child social services system that has existed for hundreds of years on the off chance that a community mental health system and foster care network will miraculously spring up to replace it. The truth is that the services we provide, while valued, appreciated, and needed by the children and families we serve, are devalued and under-appreciated by policy makers in Washington and Boston - and they have been for a long while.

No Child Left Behind will prove to be one of the great farces perpetrated on the children of this country. Held out to all of us as the panacea for improving children's performance, it has become mired in test score comparisons and labels of under performing schools for children who don't need to be ostracized any more than they already have been. It defines and mandates "highly qualified" teachers for every American classroom, a mandate that has been very difficult for states to meet.

No Child Left Behind, or *NCLB* as it's come to be called, was sold to very respected legislators on the promise that it would be accompanied by the fiscal resources to make it happen. It's not working and President Bush's legacy will be, as was his father's, a missed opportunity to improve American education.

In April of 1991 President George H.W. Bush unveiled a program called *America 2000,* in which he outlined his goals:

"By 2000, we've got to first, ensure that every child starts school ready to learn; second, raise the high school graduation rate to 90 per cent; third, ensure that each American student leaving the fourth, eighth, and twelfth grades can demonstrate competence in core subjects; fourth, make our students first in the world in math and science achievements; fifth, ensure that every American adult is literate and has the skills necessary to compete in a global economy and exercise the rights and responsibilities of citizenship; and sixth, liberate every American school from drugs and violence so that schools encourage learning."

He went 0 for 6! In August of that same year, 1991, a local newspaper published a column which said:

"The President's program will probably be a failure but not because of the components of the program outlined. The program will fail because as a nation, a state, and localities, we lack the will and desire to improve schools and the lives of the children they serve."

I wrote that 15 years ago and I'm ready to predict again that the current President Bush's *NCLB* plan will also be a miserable failure. Because government sets out a policy and outlines so-called goals doesn't make it all happen. Where both President Bushes' programs and Governor Romney's thinking on universal preschool fall short is in the failure to recognize that mandates must come with resources. *America 2000, No Child Left Behind*, and the Governor's veto of universal preschool all suggest to me a lack of foresight when it comes to children and education. If you look at education as a production line, a product rather than a process, you fundamentally misunderstand what's it's all about. There's a lot more to kids than their test scores, as those of us who are teachers and parents know.

Education policy in this country has been totally focused on products – math, science, and reading scores - with woeful lack of attention devoted to what's the best way to make improvement happen. The idea that a magic wand can be waved over kids who will then read and compute at prescribed levels is itself stupid. We know that kids learn in so many different ways that they have to be taught in varying ways as well. However the emphasis is not on methodology or technique but on the product – the outcome – the score – that you must bring up at all costs. No thought is given to "how" to do that. Just do it.

If it means declaring a large number of teachers not "highly qualified" and taking them out of the classroom with no one to follow them, that's what you do. Don't give any thought to who is going to replace them at a time when there are huge numbers of "baby boomer" teachers retiring as well. The point of it all is that, as the federal government continues to make inroads into the creation and implementation of education policy for the nation, something that didn't happen for the first 200 years of our history, things have deteriorated rapidly. As I recall, education was once a state function and for most of our history it was the states that determined curricula, teacher certification requirements, student attendance policy, and graduation requirements.

The portion of federally contributed money to most local school budgets is minuscule. More and more education is becoming a federal function, and more and more, it's a mess. We're headed toward national education standards, never the design of the Founding Fathers, but they will serve the needs of those who would homogenize American education in the name of standards. I would also note that the pressure to push DSS's *Family Networks* and like programs also emanates from federal sources, the same folks who have given us the failed *America 2000* and *No Child Left Behind*.

Policy Failure: Nothing New

Bad policy-making and implementation isn't limited to the federal government. DSS's *Family Networks* is rooted in good child welfare philosophy, but it ignores a variety of implementation realities, mostly notably the non-existence of adequate mental health and foster care systems to fill the vacuum as kids are pulled out of residential care. I can go back much further than *Family Networks* to show how state human services policy has failed miserably and ended up hurting people rather than protecting them while pursuing an idea that seemed best at the time.

I do that tonight by looking at an example of Massachusetts policy and practices set up many years ago to handle the needs of state wards, many of whom today would be supervised by DSS. The example is contained in a powerful book titled *The State Boy's Rebellion* by Michael D'Antonio.

The book tells the story of how state policy, practice, and bureaucrats not only failed to protect those in the state's care but also actively participated in their degradation, dehumanization, and humiliation. A good portion of the story takes place at the Fernald School here in Massachusetts where a young man named Freddie Boyce and others, termed "state boys" because they were wards of the state and had no families, were confined. They were there not because they were mentally retarded, as were most of the residents at Fernald. They were there because the policy makers and bureaucrats of the time embraced a theory known as "eugenics." They were there also because they were a source of free labor for the state.

Eugenics suggested that certain classes of people were inferior, shouldn't be allowed to reproduce, and, as much as possible, should be kept confined in state institutions. They were also subjected to psychosurgery, sterilization procedures, shock treatments and, later on, radioactive experiments, often done without any kind of informed consent.

When it was all over many years later, there was a lawsuit and the defendants in the case, which included the Commonwealth of Massachusetts and the United States government, both of whom were deeply involved in the scientific experiments that used the boys, paid out over $3 million in claims. D'Antonio, the author, noted that Fernald had the dubious distinction of being the center of scientific experiments on institutionalized children.

Leaving the medical experiments aside for a second, the actual treatment that the boys received, both those who were developmentally disabled and those not, was horrendous. It's all the more appalling when you think that some of these kids never should have been there in the first place, but that leaves you with the knowledge that mentally retarded children and adults were routinely treated like this.

In one particularly horrendous incident outlined at the beginning of the book D'Antonio describes a morning on the boys unit where Freddie Boyce lived during which all the boys were summarily beaten with coat hangers because one made some noise when they rose from their cots. One of the boys, Howie, who was mildly retarded, stood in line, lost control and urinated on the floor and started to cry. The attendant, enraged by that, grabbed a metal bowl and forced the other boys to urinate in it.

This is what happened next:

"…Freddie was trembling with fear, anger and a sense of foreboding…He strained to produce a stream. So did the others. When they finished, and the bowl was half-filled, (the attendant) told them to step back. She then threw the warm contents of the bowl into Howie's face."

Can you imagine! What a disgrace! The policy makers and implementers were alive and well fifty years ago. They destroyed the young lives of these children who later on were forced to rebuild what they could when they were finally released from this state-run hell hole. Lest those policy makers claim ignorance, it should be noted that that the trustees of the Fernald School were well aware that higher functioning people were housed there. Because they were cognizant of the need to have them there because of the labor they provided in the kitchen, garden, and maintenance departments, they actually, "decreed that Greene (the Superintendent) adjust admissions to make sure that at least 38 per cent of the Fernald population was composed of higher functioning children and adults. (People who today would be regarded as normal)." That was stated policy.

I recommend this book to any of you who have an interest in following what happens when bureaucracies latch on to a particular theory, in this case eugenics, and then run roughshod over those they are supposed to be protecting and serving. Bureaucracies have an incredible amount of power and, when they work well, they truly work well. But when they become zealots for a particular philosophy or way of thinking, they can stamp out the thinking proposed by others who see things differently.

Talking Truth

At the 100th anniversary of the school 10 years ago I used in a very different context one of my all time favorite vignettes about individuals who oppose the thinking of those in authority, what has become known in recent years as "talking truth to power." After he had rejected the geocentric theory of the universe which postulated that the earth was the center of all, Galileo was summoned before the church authorities, who were appalled that he would suggest that the sun, not the earth, was the center of the universe.

The Church maintained that God's creation of human beings decreed that the planet they inhabited, the earth, must be the center of the universe. How could it be otherwise? Galileo's observations suggested something very different. He believed that the *sun* was the center of the universe and that the planets moved around it. The earth was not stationary – it both rotated and revolved around the sun.

Galileo was disciplined for disagreeing with the bureaucrats and church authorities and was forced to come before them kneel, apologize, and recant what he had said, in effect to deny what his scientific conclusions were. He did as he was told. He knelt. He told them that, as they demanded, the earth was the center of the universe and then he began to rise from his knees. As he did, those nearby heard him mutter, "e pur si muove" – "but it still moves." Even if they needed to believe that the earth was the center of the universe, he had to tell them that it was not stationary. It moves.

They could make him say what they wanted. They could try to intimidate him. Maybe they could even stop making referrals to the Galileo School of Astronomy! But they couldn't make him *believe* it. "E pur si muove," "It still moves."

It's not acceptable simply to whine about things and not offer reasonable solutions. We know who we are and where we're going and we do have a place in the picture of the future. The answer to our current dilemma of governmental policies that are at odds with our work is threefold: perseverance, risk-taking, and bridge building.

Perseverance

One of my favorite stories to illustrate perseverance is one I put in the category of a "cheap laugh," something I shamelessly admit using from time to time.

A duck walks into a hardware store and asks, "got any duck food?"

"No," says the guy behind the counter. "This is a hardware store. We don't have duck food."

The next day the duck stops by again and says, "Hey, you got any duck food?"

The counterman explodes and says, "No, it's a hardware store. We don't have duck food and, if you come back again, I'll nail your little web feet to the floor."

The following day, the duck sticks his head in the door and says to the guy "hey, you got any nails?"

The guy answers, "No. We just ran out."

To which the duck responds, "Oh yeah. You got any duck food?"

That's perseverance. We have to keep at it. In this environment we must continue to concentrate on what we do and do so well knowing that over time the value of our services will again become evident. We know who we are and where we're going.

Taking Risks and Seizing Opportunities

Next, I think we have to continue to expand, take risks, and look at new and different modes of service even as our bread and butter service, residential treatment, is under attack. There's an interesting etymological issue that develops when you talk about taking risks or taking a chance. The word, chance, has two meanings – one is luck – things do happen by chance. But the other meaning is *opportunity*. In English we use the word, "chance" and we expect the listener to be able to pick up the connotation of the word from the context in which it is used. In Latin there are actually two words for chance - fortuna – meaning good fortune, luck, or by chance (the Las Vegas kind of luck) - and opportunitas – opportunity, possibility, or a chance.

If we translate the school motto, "a chance to blossom," correctly into Latin, it wouldn't be "fortuna florere," but rather "*opportunitas* florere," a chance to blossom. We're not talking about blossoming or growth coming by chance or luck around here. Rather we're saying that Perkins is a place where kids have the opportunity, or the chance, to blossom. Same word - "chance"– but a very distinct meaning.

I think of risk-taking, call it chance-taking if you will, as having very little to do with luck. It's about seizing opportunities. That's what this place is all about. We've succeeded not because of luck but because of our ability to see opportunities and to take them. We also provide opportunities for growth to kids. It's not about luck. An opportunity is a risk. We must continue to take risks and to explore what else we can do. That will not only result in expanded opportunities but will help us to better understand what we already do. T.S. Eliot said: "We shall not cease from exploration and the end of all of our exploring will be to arrive where we started and to know the place for the first time." Our current work is improved by exploring new directions.

Building Bridges

Finally, and connected to the themes of perseverance and risk-taking, I think we have to build bridges for the future of the organization and for the futures of those we serve. I am particularly committed to the construction of our child development center because it's consistent with a theme you have heard over and over – prevention.

Maybe it's an overworked analogy, but prevention is about stopping the babies from being tossed into the river rather than simply plucking them out. The bridge building I'm talking about is not the hand-holding, partnership context that those words often have. I'm talking about building bridges for the future, building bridges for those who come after us, in this case babies and young children. Prevention and early intervention hold out greater prospects for success than after the fact treatment, as important as that is.

It's the kind of bridge building described in the poem, *The Bridge Builder,* by Will Allen Dromgoole about an old man who crosses a river and then decides to build a bridge for those who will follow. He's asked:

"Old man!" Said a fellow pilgrim near.
"You're wasting your time building here,
Your journey will end with the ending day,
You never again will pass this way.

You've crossed the chasm deep and wide
Why build this bridge at even tide?"
The builder lifted his old grey head.
"Good friend, in the path I have come he said,

There follows after me today
A youth whose feet must pass this way.

This chasm which has been as naught to me,
To that fair-haired youth may a pitfall be,
He too must cross in the twilight dim,
Good friend, I'm building this bridge for *him*."

The Right Way

In these unsettled times it's all about perseverance, taking risks and seizing opportunities, and building bridges for the future. It's also about being true to who we are, constructing our world-view based on what we observe, being reasonable with those who don't view things the same way as we do, and never denying or compromising what we believe about those we serve.

Family Networks and *No Child Left Behind* are here to stay. Some of what they are trying to accomplish is good, but some elements of both will need to be modified if they are to succeed. The policy makers and bureaucrats will get their way. They always do – in the short term. But that doesn't make them *right*. The truth and the right way always seem to come out later on.

Think about Freddie Boyce at Fernald and how he waited all those years to be proven right and for justice to triumph over state mistreatment. Think about Galileo and how he wouldn't be ground down by those who dictated what the view of the world should be.

The right way always becomes clear - even if it's years later. In the short term the powers that be get want they want – it's called compliance. But in the long run, the best way, the truth, the clear path will be opened up. For us the path is perseverance, risk-taking, and building bridges.

Maybe you can make everyone agree and genuflect to the latest bureaucratic theory, whether it's *Family Networks or NCLB,* or maybe you can even force them to say the sun revolves around the earth - but there are still going to be some who will quietly reply, "e pur si muove," - "it still moves."

Eulogies

Charles P. Conroy
1920-2002

After I wrote Charles P. Conroy, 1920, dash, 2002 at the top of this page, I was reminded of something I heard not long ago. Of the three elements of the date, it's neither the date of birth nor the date of death that's important, rather it's the *dash*. The dash is the lifetime – and quite a life it was!

I'm also reminded of a comment Dad made to me in December 1999 as we all prepared for the new millennium. Somehow he had the idea that, when Mom's gravestone was carved for her in 1989, his own name was also carved with 1920, his year of birth, a dash, and then a 19 for the first two digits of a death date. His comment to me right around Christmastime, 1999 was, "Well, if I can just hang on till the end of the month, you're gonna have to do a little editing."

He was born on 36th St and never really departed from his roots. According to Charlie Conroy anyone who lived North of 59th St. was a "farmer." What you put in your car was not oil. It was "erl." My mother was a "Derl" (Doyle). The bathroom commode was a "terlet." No apologies for any of it. Nothing put on. Nothing fancy.

He did side-splitting routines about those who came in from Jersey with "the egg money" to gawk at the Empire State Building and other mammoth structures which long ago had ceased to impress him. To the love of his life he remarked on more than one occasion, "Mary, you were from 33rd Street and I was from 36th – you married up!"

I remember reading a letter he wrote to the *New York Times*, thankfully never published, in which he inquired why St. Gabriel's Park on 35th St and First Avenue had been re-named to reflect the patron of the new Armenian Cathedral on the corner of 34th and 2nd Avenue. Clearly miffed that the name of his old church, now the gaping opening of the Queens-Midtown Tunnel was gone, and that this change reflected the power of an up and coming ethnic group, Dad inquired, "and who the hell is St. Vartan anyway?"

Written correspondence as you well know is not something that was foreign to him. I recently came across an interesting piece he wrote. This particular letter was addressed to Timothy S. Healy, Director of the New York City Public Library, at its Main Library headquarters on 42nd Street. For those of you who might have forgotten, Tim Healy was an accomplished Jesuit priest who headed the library after a distinguished career as the president of Georgetown University.

Charlie regaled Fr. Healy with stories of working in the stacks of the library, and recounted how, as a young man on Thanksgiving Day with only a short time to eat, he raced from 42nd and 5th home to 34th and 3rd where he had his holiday dinner and then raced back on a full stomach. He ran not to save the nickel on the trolley but because he knew he'd simply never make it if he used any means of transportation other than his own legs.

In the course of the letter to Father Healy, he says, of two fellow library workers:

> "Two fellows pursued medical degrees: Irv Kartus, a Jewish guy, had to commute to Edinburgh for an education, and Abe Abrahamson made it domestically at a very advanced number of years (through) true grit and perseverance. They both envied my Irish puss which might have gotten them into a WASP Medical School like Cornell or Columbia."

I think that in many ways this is a window into his thinking. He was a dyed-in-the-wool New Yorker, one who understood ethnic politics, but one who also had an innate sense of fairness and believed that people should be treated well regardless of advantages or disadvantages of birth or ethnicity.

His attitudes were also the product of the three years he spent in India during the Second World War where he saw how cheap life was. He talked about mothers shooing the flies off babies, the filth in the streets of New Delhi, and it was clear that those years had quite an effect on him. He loved underdogs, the little guy, and didn't like to see people get shoved around by the more powerful.

He'd tell you it took him seven years to get through high school. We all knew that was a product of his varied interests rather than his intellectual capacity, which was huge. He was smart as hell and, if he could sucker you with the "it took me seven years to get through high school" routine, then he had you right where he wanted you.

Any number of district and regional sales managers in the Eastman Kodak Company found that out the hard way. Fresh off the plane from Wisconsin, Minnesota, or some other rural outpost that failed to garner Charlie's respect, these "managers," (whom Dad routinely referred to as "plow jockeys," befitting their humble farm roots) got worked over so badly and so quickly that they never knew what the hell hit them.

Kevin told me yesterday that he spoke to Jim Donoghue, one of Charlie's partners in crime at Kodak, who related a characteristic story about his disdain for corporate America and his distaste for any recognition that the higher ups might offer him. It should be noted that he was the first salesman in the New York region and maybe even the country to sell $1 million back in the days when a million dollars meant something to the corporate world.

Each year Kodak held its big sales meeting at one of the exclusive inns in Montauk. Charlie hated these events and was always figuring how he could duck out when no one was looking so he could get back to Manhattan or Long Beach or wherever the real action was. On this particular occasion he was singled out for some big award by the corporate bigwigs who bestowed on him a highly sought after plaque.

He dutifully accepted his award and, when no one was looking, ducked out, and hopped on the Long Island Expressway toward home. Jim Donoghue wasn't quite as lucky and got stuck for another half-hour. By the time he got out, he realized he needed gas and pulled off the road. As he was pumping his gas, he looked over at the trash bin between the two filling pumps and there on top of the trash laid Charlie's coveted award!

He was voracious reader, a sharp-witted and caustic writer, and passed that on to his children along with his straightforward approach to life often delivered in earthy terms.

"Don't give me that," he'd say. "I invented bull----, remember?" "Be your own person and don't follow the crowd" never came out quite that way. More likely it took the form of an admonition about where you shouldn't put your nose in relation to an elephant.

He lived by example. To see him return from communion at Mass was to watch a seven-year-old receive communion for the first time, hands neatly folded, eyes ever so gently cast downward. His father died when he was young and he knew what he missed and made sure his own kids never would.

He extended himself to others who needed help. My mother's mother, who was not her biological mother, lived with us for years in our apartment in Manhattan. His own mother, our grandmother, lived with us on Davidson Avenue, as did my mother's nephew, while his mother was recovering from heart surgery. Even a local kid from the East Side lived with us in the Bronx when his family situation warranted him being away for a while.

He loved an active household and, truth be told, he grudgingly admired his sons who got in and out of mischief using the street smarts and wits they gained on the East Side. That only came out as we matured.

In the heat of fire he expected good behavior. He rarely got it – but he let you think he was appalled by something you did when you knew it was minor league compared to stuff he probably did earlier. He was proudest when he walked down the aisle with his only daughter, herself something of a miracle following first of its kind heart surgery in the early 1950's.

In his last years, his kindness to others was generously returned to him as Kevin cared for his every need. He reveled in the growth and successes of his grandchildren whom he inquired about interminably.

When they lifted him out of bed last Sunday, his dry, unyielding sense of humor re-surfaced. As the nurse directed the mechanical lift that had elevated him from the bed and swung him toward a nearby chair, she instructed the orderly to let the hydraulic force out easily so he would settle gently into the chair. Instead, he mistakenly pushed it. It jerked, descending for one moment very quickly, then stopping abruptly.

Only a New Yorker who remembered the famous parachute jump ride could relate to Dad's comment as the lift bounced him up and then down, one leg only half there and the other withered to one third its size.

"Hey," said Charlie, "it's like Coney Island!"

I laughed. The orderly looked perplexed. He just didn't get it.

Dad would embarrass us as young male adults by stopping you when you were going out with your friends, grabbing both sides of your face, and kissing you right square on the face in front of your buddies. I was mortified until one of them said to me one day, "wow, *my* father never did that."

I conclude in much the same way I began using Dad's own words to help us bring it all into perspective. He and Mom came to visit us for a weekend in Lancaster in January, 1989. By then it was pretty clear that she was nearing the end of her journey although it would be eight more months before that happened. He wrote me a note which I found after they left. It said:

"I'd rather switch places but that's out of the question. She keeps telling me 'how much I have to live for.' I'm oriented in another direction because, if there's no Mary, I'm really not interested and it's no big deal hanging around. We've had a great time. I was blessed from day #1 – great parents, brothers, sisters, aunts, and uncles - the whole bit. A little growing up and learning, experiences like India – separation from Mary, my fiancée, for 3 years only made me more in love with '<u>my</u> Mary.'

"Then a batch of kids with grandmas and nanas to boot! You couldn't buy what I've had and am still having. I can't even remember the bad times – they were quick and fleeting, kind of like "testing 1-2-3." Everyone's doing great.

"Mary and Cha-Cha (have) done their thing. Still available for quick service but no big deal(s). I know how sweet life is and I've seen how cheap it can be in other parts of the world. Winning sweepstakes or lotteries make problems for guys like us. Just enough - little less sometimes and a little more others. A little struggle made the partying better when it happened. I'd gladly continue as cook, bottle washer, chauffeur, go-fer - whatever – every day's a bonus.

"Love, Dad. P.S. My prayer is you do as well!"

He re-echoed some of those themes and also some of his other strongly held convictions in a letter he wrote to Dr. Kevin Morrissey, Mom's surgeon, after her death in September 1989. He said:

"I'm lonely and struggling with lots of memories but I have no complaints over the long haul. God should be as good to everyone - but the weakest need the most attention, so I was lucky he was so compassionate."

He said it better than any of us could: Life isn't cheap; love your family; take care of one another; and especially take care of those who need you to take care of them.

He said it. He wrote it. But, most importantly, he lived his life that way.

And quite a life it was!

Katherine E. Perkins
1927-2005

The first time I met Kathy and Bud Perkins was shortly after I arrived in Lancaster. I drove up to Squam Lake to visit them at Rockywold-Deephaven Camp. They were hoping to show me that day how the lake's ice was cut for the following summer's guests.

But it was raining that day and, as you all know, (but I certainly didn't) you don't cut ice when there's rain and sleet. Coming from the East side of Manhattan the only thing I knew about ice was that when it was underfoot you poured salt and sand on it or, more appropriately, it was the first ingredient followed by a squeezed lime in a properly constructed gin and tonic.

The day was by no means a loss however. I was fortunate to meet two of the most loving and fascinating people I have ever had the pleasure to meet. We had lunch that day - a lunch that Kathy made – an indescribably good hearty New England beef stew - and there was nothing like it on that cold, raw and damp New Hampshire day. The stew was filled with vegetables and meatballs and it really hit the spot.

We talked and talked and I had a wonderful time, although as you can imagine, I regretted not being able to stand out on the lake freezing in the sleet as Bud Perkins enjoyed himself cutting blocks of ice. I remember how I felt on the ride back knowing I had just met two of the all too few people you meet in your lifetime who are truly special.

Kathy Perkins was a lot like that stew – steadfast, humble, full of inner strength, fundamental, not a lot of frills – just like good beef stew – and, oh, so good for you. And she was good for all who met her.

When you were around her, she made you feel like you were the center of the universe – never her. When you left her, the afterglow, like that beef stew, fortified and enriched you. When Kathy Perkins greeted you with a hug and a kiss - trust me - you knew you'd been hugged and kissed. There was nothing restrained or gentle about it. It was strong, demonstrative love and nobody did it better.

Whenever I called the house the conversation invariably went like something like this:

"Hi Kathy, it's Charlie. How are you?" I'd asked.

"I'm beautiful!" came her trademark reply.

If she was sitting down in the pool lobby at Perkins School and I came out of the locker room, she'd say, "hello darlin," and she didn't give a damn who heard it.

She was quite a lady – a model wife and mother, nurse, devoted friend, model Christian - on and on it goes. We mourn her but at the same time we celebrate a life well lived.

There is deep sorrow today but there should also be incredible joy for all of us who knew this very special, down to earth, wonderful lady who gave and gave - and in the process took very little. Of course the joy of having known her is more than tinged with the sorrow and loss we feel. But we can't lose sight of how much she brought to others.

When I saw her a few weeks ago at the house she was getting around very slowly. She was clearly uncomfortable but had no intention of letting me know that. I asked how she was doing. That broad, wonderful smile came across her face and, as she stood there leaning on her cane, she said, "I'm doing great, now that I see you, darlin!"

Amazing. She didn't want me to leave feeling badly for her, so she put it back on me and made me feel like I had brightened her day. She had an uncanny, unique way of doing that.

She didn't concentrate on her personal circumstances in the moment but on *you* – whoever you happened to be. She put aside her own feelings, emotions, and personal circumstances to make sure you felt better every time you encountered her.

I was privileged to have known her as a friend who embodied all the characteristics of a great mother. She was the epitome of selflessness and generosity in a world that often de-values or simply doesn't understand either.

For Kathy the best is still to come. In this church were she spent so much time and to which she was so dedicated, you have heard many biblical entreaties and hortatory comments about the good that awaits those who are selfless, true and faithful servants.

One of those biblical passages is one from Paul's Letter to Timothy in which he underscored how those who are true to the basics, who love others, who complete the course, and keep the faith are to be rewarded. In some ways it's really a condensed story about how the "beef stew" people will ultimately triumph.

This passage is emblematic of the life of Kathy Perkins – the lady who did it all right - the lady who cared for others like few others have been able to.

While you have heard this passage before, you've probably never heard it proclaimed by a Catholic in a proud Unitarian church in the language of St. Jerome's translation of the New Testament. But you will resonate to it when you hear it the way you've heard it before.

"Bonum certamen certavi, cursum consummavi, fidem servavi, in reliquo reposita est mihi justitiae corona, quam reddet mihi Dominus in illa die iustus iudex."

"I have fought the good fight, I have run the race, I have kept the faith. Henceforth there awaits for me a crown of righteousness, which the Lord, rightful judge that he is, shall give me on that day."

As we here both mourn and rejoice, at this moment Kathy is receiving that well-deserved crown. As she does, the lady who mastered the fundamentals of Christian love and service, who gave like few others, who was so conscious of others, and rarely conscious of herself, hears from God.

"Welcome good and faithful servant. How are you doing?" says the Good Lord.

To which Kathy swiftly answers, "I'm beautiful!"

She was.

(Not delivered as eulogy at service but sent to Franklin H. Perkins, Jr.)

Sonja Bernier
1940-2006

Faith

Early in my career at Perkins, after some situation concluded exactly as I had predicted, I turned to Sonja, who initially had her doubts that it would turn out the way it did, and I immodestly, and mistakenly, proclaimed, "Oh, ye of little faith."

Was *that* ever the wrong thing to say!

"I have faith and I have *always* had faith," she responded very directly.

I knew Sonja meant business, unlike other times when she waved me off in my minutes of pique and frustration, and in total disregard for the conventions of political correctness, said, "there, there, now, Doctor - don't worry your pretty little head about it."

We went back and forth in the office on which theology ruled: Sonja's "God will always provide" thinking or my tendency to believe that, "God helps those who help themselves." My suspicion is that hers was the dominant philosophy. Faith was very important to Sonja.

I never again, even in jest, critiqued Sonja's faith, which we all know was legendary, rock-solid and, frankly, an inspiration to the rest of us. In the past few years, as she cared for Ross and as she saw her own health deteriorating, she also showed us that, even in the face of great challenge, despair was never an option. Along with faith, there's always hope.

Hope

Back in January on one gorgeous afternoon after a rainstorm, itself an unusual occurrence for mid-winter Lancaster, an amazing rainbow appeared, arced over the Janeway Center in the middle of the Perkins campus. It was a little after 4pm and I was on my way back over to the house. I ran in, grabbed my digital camera, snapped a picture of this incredible spectrum of color, and e-mailed it to Sonja who was still in the office. She was having a particularly difficult time right then and she was increasingly more uncomfortable as her illness progressed. The e-mail she returned after viewing the rainbow said a lot about hope.

"Yes," she wrote. "There is a God. I've made myself a print. Marvelous." She continued, "Of course, I think the message was especially for me for I am a sick puppy and have been crying out to God for 7 days."

"I e-mailed back, "This could be what you were waiting for."

She answered with, "Or at least a sign that there is something for me at the end of my storm."

Today, she is at peace and at the end of her storm.

Sonja Bernier was a woman of great *faith*, and someone who clearly demonstrated, when others would have easily given up, that *hope* conquers all. Throughout the last 20 years she was confronted with more challenges to mind, body, and spirit than most of us ever see in a lifetime. The loss of her 2 sons, Jeff at 14 years of age and, then, Ross in 2004, both under very tragic circumstances, as well as her own health difficulties of the last few years, were amazing tests of her faith and hope.

In the face of those challenges most people would have found their faith tested, shaken, and, indeed, would have lost hope. It's easy to despair in the face of never-ending tests, but with Sonja there was never the slightest indication that her faith was shaken. She never doubted at all. She kept the faith and - with Sonja - there was always hope.

Love

However, while she was a woman of deep faith and unshakeable hope, above all she was a woman of *love*. Her care, devotion, and dedication to Ross during his time of tribulation and distress serve as a model of unconditional love.

St. Paul tells us that, as great as faith is, and as important as hope is, the greatest of the three is love. He says:

> "Love is patient, love is kind. It does not envy, it does not boast, it is not proud. It is not rude, it is not self-seeking, it is not easily
> angered, it keeps no record of wrongs. Love does not delight in evil but rejoices with the truth. It always protects, always trusts, always hopes, always perseveres.
> "Love never fails. But where there are prophecies, they will cease; where there are tongues, they will be stilled; where there is
> knowledge, it will pass away…And now, these three remain: faith, hope and love. But the greatest of these is love."

A Message

I learned my lesson when I made the flip crack about "ye of little faith." I wasn't about to make the same mistake again. I could never tell Sonja anything about faith, hope, or love - she being the epitome of all three. However, what I can do is hold her out for all of us - but especially to her two grandsons - as a model of someone who embodies all three and devotion to family as well.

And therein lies a message for all of us, but maybe more so for her two grandsons, Ross and Zach. What I hope you two boys take with you today is that your Dad struggled to find the right way and - *every* day he did that - he had the support of your grandmother.

Her love was enduring, supportive, and came with no strings attached. Your dad was a good person who had more thrown at him than most men do. He worked hard at his job. He worked hard to be a good father. He worked hard to be a good man.

In all those things he was supported, especially when times were difficult, by a mother who never gave up. When he made a mistake, she forgave him. When he faltered, she helped. When he stumbled, she picked him up. She never - ever - gave up. I think that's what kept him going – this mother of faith, hope, and above all, love.

Everyone's Mother

At Perkins, Sonja was mother to *everyone* – kids, staff, parents, me – everyone with whom she came in contact. My guess is that she played a similar role here at the Church she so loved. She tried to commiserate with those in pain or having difficulty. She loved to stay and have dinner with the kids especially on Friday nights years back in the days when she put together her campus-wide newspaper, the "What's Up Doc?" There never will be another Mrs. Santa Claus quite as authentic as Sonja's rendition.

She always had a kind word for people looking for help or solace who came to the office. They found out talking to her was a lot better than talking to me. People left more satisfied. She immediately connected with people because she was so kind. Almost from the beginning my foster son, Jay, was never just, Jay. When he called on the phone, she'd announce, "Doc - it's Sweetums."

I'm not sure if things were ever really the same after December 2, 2004, a Friday, when she went home and found that Ross's long and difficult struggle had ended and that he was at long last at peace. She, too, was remarkably at peace when she called me the next morning to report his passing – so serene, so accepting - so faithful, so hopeful, so loving.

To Ross and Zach I say: You are made of the same stuff. Love each other. Love your family. Honor the memory of your father and also honor the memory of this remarkable woman, your grandmother. Look back fondly on the best times you had with your Dad. Remember the good times and, if you are momentarily drawn to the days that were difficult, balance them with the vivid memory of your grandmother, his mother, whose love had no bounds and who loved him unconditionally. I can tell you she loved you as much.

While St. Paul tells us that the greatest of the three virtues is love, we also know that there is something exceptional, maybe even extraordinary, about a *mother's* love. It is strong, enduring, and looks for nothing in exchange. It is a love that gives life and then does all it can to support it.

A Mother's Love

A mother's love, the strength it gives to those loved, and the example it gives to those who can see it is rarely replicated in human experience. It's boundless. It's unconditional. It's a unique mixture of faith, hope and love itself.

It surpasses misery. It conquers pain. It is immortal. It, truly, can never die.

A poet, Helen Steiner Rice, summed up a lot of what many of us have seen and been inspired by these last few years as we watched Sonja live her life, take care of Ross, and boldly face her health challenges. This woman of faith and hope was, first and foremost, a woman of love, but, more importantly, a model of exactly what this poem is titled, "A Mother's Love."

> A mother's love is like an island
> In life's ocean vast and wide,
> A peaceful, quiet shelter
> From the restless, rising tide.
>
> A mother's love is like a fortress
> And we seek protection there
> When the waves of tribulation
> Seem to drown us in despair.
>
> A mother's love is sanctuary
> Where our soul can find sweet rest
> From the struggle and the tension
> Of life's fast and futile quest.
>
> A mother's love is like a tower
> Rising far above the crowd,
> And her smile is like the sunshine
> Breaking through a threatening cloud.
>
> A mother's love is like a beacon
> Burning bright with Faith and Prayer
> And through the changing scenes of life
> We find a haven there....
>
> For a mother's love is fashioned
> After God's enduring love,
> It is endless and unfailing
> Like the love of Him above.
>
> For God knew in His great wisdom
> That he couldn't be everywhere,
> So - he put His (little) Children
> In a loving mother's care.

Amen.

About the Author

Charles P. Conroy, Ed.D. is Executive Director of Perkins in Lancaster, MA, a comprehensive human service agency serving children, adults, senior citizens and their families in a variety of day, residential, and clinical services at community-based and campus-based settings. He also teaches in the graduate program in Educational Leadership and Management at Fitchburg State College in Fitchburg, MA. He is the father of Melissa, an attorney, and Janet, a social worker, and foster father of Jay.

Acknowledgments

The author expresses his sincere gratitude for the following excerpts: The Hogwarts School song from *Harry Potter and the Sorcerer's Stone* by J.K. Rowling; Elie Wiesel on "Indifference" (remarks at a White House Symposium in 1999); "Del otro lado de la noche" by Francisco Alarcon; "Gone But Not Forgotten" author unknown; "Who Will Cry for the Little Boy" from *Finding Fish* by Antwone Fisher; "De amor oscuro" by Francisco Alarcon; Description of his father by Pete Hamill; "Courage" (Boston Globe) by Yeison Quinceno; "The Bridge Builder" by Will Allen Dromgoole; and "A Mother's Love" by Helen Steiner Rice.